Islands of the Soul

Islands of the Soul

A Guide to Personal Truth and Happiness

Victoria L. Tunnermann

Writers Club Press
San Jose New York Lincoln Shanghai

Islands of the Soul
A Guide to Personal Truth and Happiness

Writers Club Press
an imprint of iUniverse.com, Inc.

For information address:
iUniverse.com, Inc.
5220 S 16th, Ste. 200
Lincoln, NE 68512
www.iuniverse.com

ISBN: 0-595-14834-4

Printed in the United States of America

I dedicate this book to my family; to my husband and undoubtedly my best friend, Chuck, for his unfaltering love and encouragement, to our daughter Raven, and to all of the animals with whom we have chosen to share our lives. And for my father, Ronald, who never passed up a good book.

Introduction

This book was written as the result of communication established between my husband and me, and two separate personalities, "Pete" and "Mejik", who first corresponded with us through the use of an oracle board. We refer to Pete and Mejik by name because names are actually tools by which we connect, or reconnect, to those energies that exist within and around us. When we desire to be close to another human being we call out to them. And when we desire to be in touch with the energies that exist within and around us, we have the capability of calling out to them as well. However we prefer to name those energies is decided by the way that we perceive reality. Whether we prefer to label them as souls that have passed over, spirit guides, or energies with distinct personalities known as Pete and Mejik, they are all valid and they are all easily available to us, provided we take the steps necessary to reconnect with them.

For those who might be apprehensive about establishing connections through an oracle board, or any other means for that matter, I have written this book. Because of the positive connections that my husband and I have experienced, I felt it was important to help others who desire to make their own positive connections to the energies within and around them.

I have read many books and performed countless hours of research into the realm that exists beyond this physical existence. In doing so, I quickly became aware that certain individuals felt left-out of this realm. Whether it was because of confusion early on, or because they were warned of the dangers of delving into a world that was somewhere beyond their own, they shied away from the experience. But what it is important for each person to understand, is that the only danger that exists is the danger associated with *not* experiencing the happiness that comes with the sense of connection to our energies.

You do not have to be "psychic" in order to connect to your energies and reap the rewards that they can offer. Anyone is capable of re-establishing ties to the energies that exist within and around them. As you will come to understand when you read this book, you have never really been without these energies. They are always present, but it is up to you to make the decision whether to establish communication with them or ignore them. Since they are a part of your self (as all energy is connected) it is to your advantage to allow them to give you their timeless wisdom.

For those who are not completely aware of the ways in which the energies of the spirit world operate, I offer some of my own experiences as a reference. Some individuals who read this will see parallels between my experiences and their own. Others will undoubtedly have had personal experiences that are not discussed here, but which are just as important. What we all must realize is that each time we observe our personal definition of a "coincidence", "deja-vous", or even something as potent as a "miracle", we are in touch with the energies that allow certain individuals to be termed "psychic". And if these individuals can utilize these energies in such a way as to understand the workings within themselves and others, there is no reason to doubt that you can attain this natural state as well.

Although I often did not use the correct words to describe my experiences, I had always been aware of my psychical talents. Other than reading Tarot cards and preparing Astrological charts, I had had many experiences with energies, or as some would prefer to call them, "the spirit world". Sometimes these contacts came through dreams or the altered state of consciousness that I drifted into as I prepared for sleep. Other times these energies contacted me while I was wide awake.

As a child I knew when things were going to happen. I did not have, or perhaps never developed, the ability to see spirits or energies while I was awake, but the feelings and messages I received, during both my sleeping and waking hours, were always accurate.

By the time I was a teenager, I had read every book and watched every movie that even remotely included some element of the spirit world. As I read or watched, I noticed that I was being guided in a clear and precise direction. I do not wish to infer that another entity was in control, only that my energies were in sync with other energies that held the same ideas and truths that I held. Work with these energies helped lead me to books that were correct for me, and from these books I was able to gain contacts with other authors or groups that encouraged my spiritual growth.

I was not the only person in my family however, to display any sort of psychic awareness. My father and a few other relatives had these gifts to varying degrees, but none of them chose to develop them. My father, for example, had the ability to sense when there were unhappy or negative energies around, or when something bad was about to happen. I do not believe that this was the only psychic ability he had, but it was the only one he chose to allow to come to the surface. He recognized that he had this gift, but chose not to delve far enough within himself to examine the source. Had he gone this route, he probably would have mastered an understanding of many different types of occurrences instead of the very narrow field that he allowed his senses to decree. But he was satisfied with his ability as it was, and therefore it was not up to me or anyone else to attempt to change that. This was his personal Truth (more about this in the book).

Over the years I became aware that whenever I denied the spiritual side of myself (by "spiritual", I do not mean "religion", but the energy that is within us, connecting us to all energy, both in this world and in others) I did not meet with as many psychical occurrences. The less involved I was in spirit, the more I had to work for my contacts. As soon as my contacts were reestablished, the energy flowed freely.

Shortly before I was married, my husband (fiancée at the time) and I bought a Ouija Board at, of all places, a local toy store. My work with readings, which now included past-life readings, had expanded. Along with this expansion, came my contacts with the spirit world. In an attempt to focus on one main source from which all others could correspond, thus making things easier, (or so I thought) we picked up the board.

Neither one of us had any reservations about working with the board. My husband, who is a very spiritual person as well, agreed with my feelings that the board was not a tool to fear. He, like I, believes that the type of energy that each of us puts out is the same energy that we will receive. So when we started working with the board, we did so with confidence.

We attempted to make contact with our "main source" on January 8, 1995. I will admit that after fifteen minutes of jumbled words and letters, we started to wonder if we could make this work. But we never gave up. Approximately one half hour into our attempt we received a name; "Nepudhot 1." At first we thought that these letters were part of the menagerie we had received earlier, but then the planchette moved over the same letters again. We asked a few questions in an effort to "test" whatever we had contacted, asking permission aloud before proceeding. At one point I concentrated on a color and left my husband in charge of the planchette. The pointer spelled out the color I was thinking of at the time, and continued to predict other colors with complete accuracy. We attempted similar tests, all with the same results. We then asked whatever we had contacted to reveal a little about themselves. The following script is taken from our first encounter with our friend, "Nepudhot 1", also known as "Pete".

FIRST CONTACT WITH PETE, JANUARY 8, 1995.

(Note: Quotation marks around Pete's words, and punctuation, have been added for easier reading. Contained within each set of quotes is a full thought which occurred before the planchette paused and Pete began a new one.)

"Year died 4717. You see this year as 1995, I see it as 18284." (We went over these numbers twice.)

We asked if he had ever lived on this Earth.

"19 Earthly existences."

"1726 your time. Time of last existence. You knew me as Pete."

Our first several meetings with Pete proved very informative. Both my husband and I received personal information, all of which proved to be true. We also received information that we had known was true in our hearts even without having concrete evidence to back it up. (Examples of this nature are those meetings with Pete that pointed out our past lives. Almost all of these were existences that we had suspected we had lived, even before Pete brought them to our conscious attention.)

My husband and I enjoyed our time "speaking" with Pete, and made it a point to meet with him a few times every month. During these meetings we gained an understanding of Pete's personality. His energy clearly showed a sense of humor, as well as a broad range of intelligence. He proved to be very patient and would move the planchette to "Good-Bye" if he felt our energy waning, rather than jeopardize our physical and emotional states.

When my husband and I purchased a Third-Eye Board about six months later, we noticed that Pete's messages came through much easier and more clearly. The planchette moved more freely, and we began to experience true conversation instead of stop-and-go sentences. It was during one of the initial meetings through the Third-Eye Board that Pete introduced us to Mejik.

During this particular meeting I had been inquiring about one of my past-lives. Pete answered most of my questions, but let it be known that there was another source of energy with which I would benefit from working. His exact words of introduction were, "Call her Mejik." (We checked this spelling twice.)

Mejik's energy came through immediately. She greeted us with, "Delighted to be here." And from that moment on, contact with her has been an absolute delight for both my husband and myself.

Through meetings on the Board and through my own experiences with automatic writing, we have learned new ways of looking at the world. We have also re-learned many of the things that this physical existence has tempted us to forget. But as happy as we felt, as spiritually aware as we had become, we realized that we could not be selfish with the information we were receiving. Books that we had read, and television programs that we had watched, pertaining to the subject of human spirituality, failed to mention the essence of what we had learned through our meetings with Pete and Mejik. We wondered why so many individuals had disconnected from the part of themselves that would help them understand and live these teachings. As Pete once mentioned in a meeting in 1995, "Remembering is merely time forgotten," and based on this statement, we realized we were not the only ones who were capable of "remembering", or reconnecting. If it took Pete and Mejik's energy to help us remember, we felt it was our duty to take the next step and share the information we received with the world.

In April 1998, my husband and I met with Pete and Mejik and told them of our intentions. Since they were the source of our remembering, we felt it only right that they should have a say in whether we should share the information with the rest of the world through this book. They whole-heartedly agreed, even joking about the "project" that we had in store for them. And so the book you are about to read took flight.

My husband and I poured over pages and pages of notes from our meetings with Pete and Mejik. Our handwritten notes contained a lot of personal information that had to be omitted before we made an attempt at narrowing the information we wanted to share. Pete's suggestion was to write about the Seven Islands he had re-introduced us to in past meetings.

These Seven Islands of the Soul; Quality, Love, Knowledge, Beauty, Balance, Perception, and Nothingness must emerge in all of us in order to live in a state of absolute Truth, and therefore happiness. (Perhaps you are familiar with the saying, "Be true to yourself"? Well, this is what we mean.)

The ability to get back in touch with these seven centers (Islands) within us, makes us each happier, more fulfilled, and ready to relate to the world with a renewed sense of ourselves and our Truths. Once we understand the meanings of our personal Islands, we are better able to see where in the past we have allowed others, against our personal sense of Truth, to make choices for us.

To visit your Islands and draw from the energy within them (the energy that exists as a result of your personal Truth) is akin to being reborn. The feelings that you once felt in association with going against your sense of Truth will no longer exist for you. Your choices will be your own, and your values and senses will not be compromised as a result of outside influences. If you take the time that is necessary (don't hurry through!) to comprehend the meaning of each Island as it is described in this book, you will finish it a truly happier spirit.

This book is meant to be a teaching tool. It is meant to help those who read it to recognize and develop their own "truths", and to encourage this development in others. Because the lessons within each Island are the basis for Truth, I felt it best to divide the book into seven sections. The book does not read like a conversation. Aside from a few exceptions, there are no quotation marks to indicate where Pete and/or Mejik spoke. But the words, the philosophies and ideas behind them, and the Seven Islands themselves, are inherently theirs. I, as the author, took the liberty of putting in the correct punctuation and forming the paragraphs necessary in writing a book.

There are times however, where I interject an opinion or comment that I feel is of importance to the reader in her/his understanding of the Islands. At those points, I use the word "I". Throughout the rest of the book, Pete and Mejik refer to their audience as both "you" and "we". These words are not meant to confuse, but to bring awareness to the reader that through our Islands, all energies are interchangeable.

I end this introduction with a quote we received from Pete when we first discussed the Islands you are about to visit.

"Release fears to open your mind's eye. Sight comes forth and clearer vision follows rebirth. 7 Islands exist in each of us. Within them we find buried treasures. Find the map and go on an adventure. Memories that have become buried are now within our reach. Find them and become rich."

THE ISLAND
OF
QUALITY

Quality is the basis of all.
Pete

The first, and undoubtedly the most important island to be discussed, is the Island of Quality. Without a true understanding of this island of the soul, one cannot move on to the other six islands and expect to reap the rewards that each is willing to extend. Because each island is actually an extension of a self that we as humans have learned to ignore, they must be reintroduced to us one at a time, and in a particular order. To skip from one island to another without quite grasping the concept of the one before, is comparable to swimming in circles. Any questions that may be raised as a result of our experience on an island, cannot be fully addressed if we go "island hopping".

Think of it this way. You have booked a much needed seven day vacation that takes you on a guided tour of a new island each day. This sounds wonderful to you because your high-pressured mind has brainwashed you into thinking that a chance to see several places during one vacation is better than being stuck on the same island day after day. And since most of us grant ourselves minimal vacation/ relaxation time, you believe that this type of vacation is what you require to feel refreshed. You treat this vacation like several vacations rolled into one, and almost make yourself feel better by convincing yourself that this makes up for any relaxation time

1

you might have missed, or will miss in the future. However, very shortly after you begin your vacation you realize that you are more stressed and more frustrated than you were before you booked your trip. There are several reasons for this.

Foremost, is the fact that you actually did not book a vacation at all, but in actuality spent your money to do the same thing you do day after day in this high-pressured life that most human beings choose to live. The geography might have changed, but your way of thinking did not. You still felt the need to rush; to try to cram every aspect of seven different places into seven days.

You also feel pressured and stressed because someone else (tour guide) is leading you around the islands. You are free to go off on your own, but then you imagine you will miss the best parts of the island and you struggle within yourself to come to terms with what you should do to make your vacation a happy one. After all, you think, you wouldn't want to go home thinking you might have missed something that you probably will never have the chance to see again. Yet, how do you know whether the best things about the island are what the tour guide is showing you, or what you might have stumbled upon had you left the group and went out on your own.

Unfortunately, the questions you face cannot be answered as long as you are following the direction of another. And this "other" manifests in your life anytime you allow your will, the source of your true happiness, to be compromised. Instead of trying to fill every second of your life with things that you feel might be better for you, stop and force yourself to take a break from the group. Realize that you are under no pressure to get from island to island in a specified amount of time. In fact, if you hurry through this book as you would through your vacation, you will have compromised yourself once again because you will have missed the deeper meaning associated with each island. You may be able to say you successfully completed your trip through the islands in this book, but you can only *report* on them based on the briefness of your stay. Wouldn't you feel much better knowing that if you took the time necessary, you could be happily *living* the lessons that this book was meant to teach you? So take your time! Saunter from island to island at your own pace. You will know it is time to move on to the next when the island that you are visiting becomes so familiar to you that it begins to reemerge within you.

As we had mentioned earlier, our first stop on our island excursion, is to the Island of Quality. Without reading ahead, try to define the things in your life that are of quality. Ask yourself where and when you most often use the word quality in your daily life. Does the word appear in your vocabulary in an effort to define material things? (i.e.: "This shirt is made of quality fabric.") Or do you find yourself using it to describe intangible things that bring true meaning and happiness into your life?

Do not try to coax yourself into believing one of these definitions is the correct one. Too many times we are forced to believe that we must follow one sequence of thought in order to be considered "correct" or a "good person". Our parents, various religions, teachers, counselors, etc., have had such an impact on us over the years that whether we realize it or not, we have grown up within a state of constant conflict. We struggle each day between what we feel we would *like* to do, and what society dictates we *should* do. We suffer as individuals when we choose to go against our will and the source of our happiness to allow others to make us feel guilty or hurt. Unfortunately, many of us decide that this is the place where we must remain. We get used to a pattern and follow it, mainly because we fear what change can bring. But we need that vacation! We need to revisit the Island of Quality within ourselves and rejuvenate. We need to examine why we think the way we do, why we feel the way we do, and how we look at ourselves and the world around us. What we desperately need to investigate is how we came to our present view of reality.

Reality is filtered through the glass of quality. Actually, reality is the direct result of quality being expressed. In other words, the way that we see and respond to the world (our personal reality) is directly connected to what we hold within ourselves as our personal "truth". In the past you may have heard the expression, "We each create our own reality." Although this is a true statement, it may have been hard for us to accept as Truth because we are conditioned to believe that there are many outside forces at work in our lives, over which we have no control. Some people refer to these forces as Fate, or even a Higher Power that is, in its infinite wisdom, supposed to know what is best for us. If this is what we ascribe to, the belief in these outside forces, then this becomes our version of reality. However, this is not a reason for us to assume everyone should share the same views of reality that we do. What each of us considers "right" or "wrong" varies from person to person. And if we look to the great diversity in our religious or spiritual beliefs, we see even more proof of a world that exists without the boundaries of one precise reality. Yet each group, religious or otherwise, and each individual being has created its own reality. Their belief systems are the direct result of what they feel from within their core; their inner judge of Quality.

Realizing this, each of us must now ask ourselves why we feel it is right to force our individual beliefs on others. If our beliefs radiate from deep within ourselves, we are doing a great injustice to our fellow human beings by attempting to invalidate their inner sense of Quality in favor of our own.

Stop for a moment and consider the attitude of one of your friends (or perhaps yourself, if the following description applies). Each of us knows at least one person who is generally "blue" and who tends to have a pessimistic outlook on their life. Because we are friends with them, we feel we have the right to tell them they are looking at the world the wrong way. We say things such as, "Snap out of it", or "Things aren't that bad". But the fact is, things *are* bad for this person. Anything we say in an attempt to force them to think otherwise is futile. Their outlook on life cannot be changed by a few words, nor should it be. Reality as they see it, cannot be altered unless they are willing to redefine their own sense of Quality, which for many people is a very scary task. It is much easier for them to live with the feelings and the attitude they have created for themselves, then to try to go deep within to the source of their negative personality. On an unconscious level they know that they are solely responsible for the way that they feel and act. But they are truly afraid of communicating with their own inner-voice; their own essence. Undoubtedly they know at some level what is good for them. However, fear keeps them from changing even the slightest bit. When we adopt fear, and allow it to assume control, we actually convince ourselves that any change would set us up for unhappiness. For example, a person whose reality is being physically ill most of the time, often will not allow themselves to become well again if there is another person in their life who lavishes them with continuous attention and affection throughout the duration of any malady. Though they may not be aware of it at a conscious level, the need for attention and uplifting emotion is actually at the root of this person's problem. They fear these things being taken away from them if they prove they are healthy. Since there is no incentive for them to rely on themselves and alter their sense of Quality, they find no reason to change their present reality. Yet, if we spoke to an individual who was like this, they would declare they did not choose to be sick. They would try their best to convince us that we should feel sorry for them, thus adding to their circle of sympathizing acquaintances. On a conscious level, they probably would not realize that this is what they were doing. Because they are so far removed from their sense of Quality, they perceive the emotional withdrawal from others as a threat. Unfortunately, they have identified so strongly with the idea that their needs must be met by outsiders, they refuse to agree with the wisdom deep within them. This wisdom, or inner voice, tells them they are the only one who can produce what they need in life because they are the sole creator of their sense of reality!

To receive loving and caring emotions from others is not a bad thing. On the contrary, the emotion and affection that we receive from others can make us feel wonderful. It should be welcomed in our lives if this is how we choose to allow ourselves to feel. However, coming to rely on these feelings from others just to feel good about ourselves is not good for us. When this happens, we should begin the process of redefining our reality to the point that we become responsible for our own happiness. This way, our needs are always met, and any additional love and affection we receive would be an added bonus for us. Our life, lived from a source of true inner happiness and love, would be a life of Quality.

Once we have connected with our personal Island of Quality we realize that we are not as isolated as the word 'island' might suggest. Although reality is different for each human being, our inner sense of Quality is universal. To tap into that source of universality enables us to connect with all things, both living and what many consider "non-living". Because all things contain energy, and exchange energy on a continuous basis, all things are indeed living to various degrees. With the exchange of energy between these living things comes the voice of knowledge that radiates from the Island of Quality. Every thing that exchanges energy becomes linked by the sands of Quality. We can best observe this in our world when we concentrate on the origins of societal trends.

When we begin to think about changing something as simple as our hairstyle, or something more complex such as the interior of our home, we are not the only ones who are feeling the stirring of much needed changes within us. As these ideas are taking shape we are actually in communication with the Islands of Quality in others around us. As we take action to change styles or colors, we recognize that our choices tend to be popular or "in" at the time. This is because the universal connection we have with others has lead us toward the same alterations. For this very reason, it is a fallacy to believe that fashion designers or artists or even advertising executives, dictate what is popular or trendy. The fact is, such people are working with the spirit (or energy) of the art. And depending on how strong that spirit/energy is, it can vanish only to reappear at a different time when the ideas it represents are more appealing. What many people would term, "ahead of their time", or "intuition", is the result of individuals being better in touch with the workings of universal Quality.

Where Quality is the issue, we are all functioning within the boundaries of the same definitions. It is through our personal sense of reality however, that we differ. Suppose the most sought-after color on the runways this year is purple. Those stores and those individuals who were in touch with the shift in universal Quality stocked up on every purple outfit they could. Some bought the most popular styles in the color purple, and others bought at least a few pieces of clothing in this color. Even those individuals who claimed they did not follow the latest fashions, incorporated more of the color into their wardrobe. As human beings, we cannot help this. We are the ones who created the popularity of the color by connecting universally. Our need for a change, whatever the reasons, may have been, prompted us to direct our energies toward something that would ultimately enhance our lives. Choosing to alter something as seemingly simple as a color may not have been such a simple decision after all. When we consider that each of us, consciously or unconsciously, is perpetually attempting to make our reality better by expressing our sense of Quality, we understand that any change, no matter how insignificant it may appear at first, is the result of our source of being crying out for something to make us feel better. Knowing this, we can reexamine our reason for choosing the new color of the season. If we chose purple, as mentioned before, we undoubtedly chose it for what it represents to us. Some may see it as the color of wisdom. Others see it for its royal attributes. To each of us, the color will represent something different. Although the color itself is universal because it was pulled from our Island of Quality, the definitions of this color vary because of our individual sense of reality.

For those who have read up to this point it is important to understand that although each of us is in tune with each other through a universal sense of Quality, we do not necessarily have to define what we see, or even what we create imaginatively in the same way. Once again, remember that our sense of reality is filtered through the Island of Quality. Because of this, we are provided with an exceptionally strong basis, but that is all.

What we choose to do with that basis, that is, how we choose to define what manifests in our world as a result of this sense, is entirely up to us. Each of us sees the world in a different way because each of us creates a different view of reality. Therefore, each symbol, each color, each and every thing in this world and in our imagination, can mean something unique for each individual.

The universality of Quality does not extend to our unique versions of reality because in this lifetime we have chosen the ability to work with freedom of choice. Those who do not believe that we have such freedom, actually contradict themselves by making such a statement. Their belief that they lack a choice, is, in their reality, a choice. They can at any time, choose to believe that they do have a choice in this lifetime, and they would then have the ability to change their present reality. But the fact that they deny this ability makes their reality what it is. Most likely, they are one of the individuals we discussed earlier; the ones who prefer to extract sympathy from others by convincing them that some force outside themselves has made it impossible for them to be happy and healthy in this world.

If you feel that you may indeed be the type of person we just mentioned, do not despair. Whatever it is that you believe, whether your faith lies in yourself or in outside forces over which you feel you have no control, something lead you to this book. Perhaps a friend offered you the chance to read it, or you just happened to like the way the cover looked and thought you might buy it. (Again, recognize that there are countless possibilities.) In both of these situations, we can see where different views of belief have come into play, yet remain neither right nor wrong, just different. To explain this, let us examine both situations from these varying view points.

Suppose you are the person who believes in the forces and energies within yourself, and you are certain that through your own efforts, you will achieve your desires. You happen to be speaking with a friend one day and your friend mentions that she has just finished reading a book that you might find interesting. She gives you this book and you begin reading it. Once you have reached this point in the book, it becomes obvious to you that your friend's sense of Quality and your own were so in tune with one another that your friend was able to decipher the message that your energies were sending, that is, how very much you would benefit from reading this book. You believe that you already have all the answers within you, and what your friend picked up on was something that existed inside you all along; something that you may have been out of touch with momentarily. Therefore, someone else (in this case, your friend) brought the book to you. Had you been in touch with what was going on in the area of Quality, you would have discovered the same book on your own. Maybe you had been concentrating on a different Island of the Soul, and so your Island of Quality called out to another for what it needed. On an inner level you always knew what you needed, but because of demands in other areas that occupied your time, your sense of Quality threw out a few hints to get you back on track. But on a conscious and an unconscious level you know, and always knew, that what happens in your life is the result of your personal energies at work.

On the other hand, let us look at the same scenario from the viewpoint of someone who does not believe that they are in control of what happens to them.

You are the type of person who believes that outside forces and energies govern your life. If you are sick, it must be because someone else gave you a cold. If you are unhappy with your present employment, you think you cannot change things because outside forces and energies might cause you to end up in a worse position. In general, you blame other people and energies outside yourself for the circumstances that exist in your life. So when your friend hands you this book to read and parts of it begin to make sense to you, your first reaction is to wonder why it took so long for this book to come into your life. You feel a little angry that you have been going through life for so long and nobody has provided you with the answers you so desperately needed. But if you have gotten this far in this book, then you probably realize what I am about to say next. The only thing that prevented you from changing the circumstances of your life earlier, was that you didn't take control from the very beginning. Your sense of Quality always knew what it needed, but you chose to override it by convincing yourself it could not be trusted. Under these conditions, Quality has no other choice than to express itself through outside forces and energies. Although it emanates from you, it understands your belief system and will do whatever it takes to make sure you receive what you need. Therefore, if you believe that what you need is outside of you, your sense of Quality will find a way to impress itself onto other people, forces, and energies so that through them, you will recognize it. If you decided to change your way of looking at things, that is, if you changed your view of reality by allowing your sense of Quality to act as the filter, you would realize you could eliminate the middle-man. You would not have to rely on others to give you what you needed if you relied on your own sense of Quality.

Although the previous example illustrates how two different people interpret an event that happened in their lives, it also serves to illustrate how nothing that happens in our lives happens without a part of us being involved in the process. We may understand things differently, but ultimately we are all functioning from the same inner core. Our senses of Quality are not the same, and therefore our sense of reality is not the same. Yet we all possess the ability to change our present reality if we so choose. We can do this by getting back in touch with our sense of Quality.

How to Gain Access to the Island of Quality

There are certain things to consider when attempting to attain closer harmony with your Island of Quality. The first question you must ask yourself is, What Is My Truth? Simply asking the question and waiting for the universe to provide you with an answer, however, is not enough. We must search our inner Island for the knowledge that we all knew at one time, but managed to suppress over the years.

Each of us possesses the ability to understand that which is our personal Truth; what makes us happy, and what we strive for within this realm of happiness. Each of us came into this world knowing what we would need to bring true happiness to our lives and the lives of those around us. But somewhere along the line we lost touch with this deep, inner knowing. The pressures of society and even our daily existence caused us to push part of what we are to the background, in favor of what we feel we need to "get by" in this physical world. Often we are taught that what we are as spiritual beings has to take second place to our job, our materialistic pursuits, or our desire to fit in with the crowd. We realize too late that when we subscribe to this way of thinking we are neglecting our inner Islands. Being accepted by society becomes our goal, and we think that what is inside of us is not enough to offer society. But when we reflect on such thoughts, we gain insight that causes us to wonder how our personal Truth can be anything but enough. This Truth sustained us as we came into this world. Yet the greatest fault exists within us when we do not listen to this part of ourselves. If the society that you live with each day is not the type of society you desire, do not try to conform by letting go of something so meaningful inside of you. Instead, learn to communicate with your inner sense of Quality and trust it to help you become what you desperately need to be. If each of us lived by this code, we would all see a radical shift in society as a whole.

At the present time, too many of us alter our thoughts and feelings to coincide with what we feel others expect from us. This is acceptable only if our actions and thoughts are the result of our personal Truth. If they are not part of this Truth, then we are living an existence that is lacking true happiness.

The fist step to finding your sense of Truth and your Island of Quality, is letting go. Take a few minutes to sit quietly and disconnect the part of your brain that finds a so-called rational explanation for everything. Let the more loving side of yourself take over. Feel the energy within your heart as you would when you embrace a person or an animal that you love, or imagine the love you feel when you witness a very emotional scene in nature. Savor these feelings within your heart and then transfer the feeling to your brain. Don't allow the rational part of your brain to convince you that these emotions are not worthy. They are a part of you; and anything that is a part of you is a very worthy thing.

Remain with this feeling for a few more minutes. Do not let it slip away quickly. If you enjoy this emotional response, know that you are entitled to stay within it for as long as you would prefer. To be able to be silent and concentrate entirely on your feelings is the first step to reaching Quality.

While you are within the feeling that you just conjured, begin to imagine all the things in your world that bring you happiness. Do not fall prey to thoughts that make you feel you must include something if you don't want to. For example, if a certain member of your family has treated you in a less than kind way, you do have the right not to include them in your list of people who bring happiness into your life. Remember, these are *your* thoughts and feelings, and they cannot be wrong.

After you have imagined all the things that bring happiness to your life, begin to imagine all the things that you have done to bring happiness to others' lives. Open up to all the energy that you are feeling at this time. This is good, positive energy that is now breaking through the cracks.

Picture this energy moving throughout your being. There is no one correct way to imagine it. You need not view it as white energy, or blue energy, or as circles, dots, or little hearts. The truth is, this is *your* energy, and you should see it any way that you wish. The only important thing is that you sense it.

Once the energy has moved through you, pay attention to where it comes together. The sensation of moving energy should last anywhere from a few seconds to a few minutes, so do not feel rushed. When the energy has reached its destination, make note of it. This is the energy of Quality. The place within yourself that you feel this energy most strongly will tell you precisely from where your sense of Quality, and therefore reality, is derived.

If your energy comes to rest at your eyes, this is telling you that your sense of Quality is based upon what you see. Your reality is based on being shown things, or gaining proof before you believe. You find it hard to accept someone's word on something without seeing the physicality of what they are saying for yourself. However, if your energy rested between your eyes, at the sight of your third-eye, this indicates that you do *not* need to see things in order to believe them. You trust that which cannot be proven wholly by the five senses we were taught we possess. Your reality encompasses not only the world you live in, but the world which you cannot see or sense in the conventional ways. You have dream experiences, and have encountered spirits from other existences. But because your energy is focused in the area known as a third-*eye*, you experience these things most often through the sense of sight. You have vivid dream images, for example, or you have actually *seen* visions from other worlds.

If your energy rested on your hands, then you are they type of person who needs to do things for themselves. You rarely trust anyone else to get things done, knowing that you are the only one who can do the type of job you want done. You do not trust your other senses as much as you trust your sense of touch. You need to have tangible proof of things in order to believe.

To have energy centered around your heart means that you need to *feel*. You can see something with your eyes, hold it in you hand, even smell it, and if it doesn't feel the way it is supposed to, you cannot believe it is what it is supposed to be. You are not the type of person to believe what others tell you simply because they believe it. You must feel the truth of the matter within your heart in order to be satisfied. You are also a sensitive person. You understand and experience other people's feelings, sometimes as though they were your own. This is often how you know they are being sincere.

You do not believe in this world alone, but in the worlds outside this existence as well. You may not see spirits or hear the voices of dearly departed loved ones, but you do feel it when other energies are near you.

These three examples of central points for energies are the most common. There are, undoubtedly, many other points where energy can accumulate. Individuals who have lost their sense of sight, for example, will sometimes feel their energy pooling around their ears if they are accustomed to relying on their sense of hearing to define reality. Anywhere that you feel energy coming together, is the point from which your Quality is defining your reality. Should you wish to change your present view of reality, start by changing the point from which your Quality makes itself known. For example, if you need proof of things in order to believe them and this has impacted on your life in a way you do not like, or no longer feel comfortable with, start imagining the energy that rested in your hands or your eyes being pulled toward a place like your heart. You should not feel the need to let all of the energy flow to a different spot right away. Many times just helping some of that energy to pool in a different place in your body will help you to create more balance.

After a short period of practicing this energy imagery, you will notice you do not feel the urgency for proof that you felt before. If you moved some of your energy to your heart, for example, you will become aware that you trust your feelings more. And if your energy shift was toward the third-eye region, you will notice you no longer feel the need to receive solid proof through the five physical senses alone.

We realize that it may be hard to shift your energy at first. Too often we let our fears dictate our lives, and prevent us from changing, even when we know that change is what we need. But do not be afraid to move at least some of your energy to another place in your body. Remember you are moving this energy because deep inside you want to change. And if you are capable of moving the energy to a new place, then you are also capable of moving it back. This is exactly why you are beginning to move your energy a little at a time. You will adjust better to the shift in your reality if you approach it slowly. If you go too fast, or decide the change is not right for you at the present time, you can always imagine the energy back where it was. Sometimes just to be able to do this is enough, as it allows you insight into your sense of Quality and explains why you think and act the way you do. The important thing to remember overall is that you are always in control. You have the power to understand what goes on inside you; and you also have the power to change those things that you want to change.

Once you truly understand the source from which your sense of Quality emanates, you are ready to move on the to next Island; the Island of Love.

THE ISLAND
OF
LOVE

The night falls only to reveal the brilliance of the moon.
Mejik

Reaching the Island of Love requires the release of fear. This release opens
your flow of creative energy. The energy that you encountered when we
visited the Island of Quality, does you little good if it remains completely
within you. For energy to be utilized correctly, it must be transferred.

Those who have experienced the feeling of anticipation that emerges
before someone you care for opens a gift that you have given them, know
the emotion associated with this Island. The energy that is within you goes
out to the other person even before you actually hand them the gift. You
begin working with transferred energy the moment you think about getting them the gift. In the following scenario, we will take you though the
places that energy is transferred between two people.

Suppose you receive an invitation to a surprise party for a good friend.
A transference of energy takes place the moment you open the invitation
and realize that the person who is throwing the party recognized the
importance of your friendship by extending you an invitation. The feelings you experience (and the place within you from which they stem)
immediately upon opening the invitation, give you a better understanding
of what your friendship with this person is based upon. Should you experience anything but happy emotions, stop for a moment to focus on the

part of your body from which the less-than-happy emotions are emanating. If, for example, your energy draws your focus to your eyes, then you are dealing with something the person did physically that you may not have liked. At this point, take note of any manifestations near the area you have focused upon. If you are wrinkling the space between your eyebrows, then you are probably dealing with anger. If you feel your eyebrows rising or your eyes becoming wider, then the basic emotion you are expressing has to do with a situation in which you felt hurt. This feeling would be accompanied by a sense of disbelief that you would be included on the list of invitees after what happened between the two of you. (More on physical reactions in places of energy, later.)

No matter what reaction you experience as a result of opening and reading the invitation for your friend's party, you have reacted to a transference of energy. How the person writing the invitation felt about you, how the person whose party it is feels about you and how you feel about them, are all channels by which energy is transferred.

In order not to stray too far from the original scenario let us pretend that you are happy to have received the invitation. Your next thought, after you read the invitation, is what to give this person as a gift. While you are contemplating this, there is a transfer of energy occurring. You are pulling from your sense of Quality any ingredients necessary to form an idea of what the person would like. Because you have tapped into your Island of Quality, this idea is based upon how you feel about them. If your friendship is such that you have always exchanged gifts with this person based on the principle, "It's the thought that counts," then you would work with the energy of your heart and your third-eye to choose an appropriate gift. The energy you would be using would be pulled from the place within you that we spoke of in the previous chapter.

When you imagine someone or something bringing happiness into your life, you are actually transferring energy between yourself and that person/animal/thing. You feel the warmth and love associated with the type of friendship you have, and you base your decision in gift-giving upon this. Even if you cannot picture the exact item that you wish to give your friend, you can understand the feeling that you get when you walk into a store to purchase the gift, or get your supplies ready to make the gift. The little questions you ask yourself are really asked of the energy that is inside you that has mingled with your friend's energy. You draw from your sense of Quality when you ask, "Would she/ he prefer blue or green?", "Should I use solid or printed fabric in what I am making?", etc.

When you visit the Island of Love, you are still working with Quality, but the Quality you use is not entirely your own. Each person who has ever touched your life has mingled with your energy in some way. Those who have impressed us in a good way are those to whom we want to give the best of our knowledge of Quality.

If we look to our last example, we come to understand why such a good friendship causes us to reach toward our highest sense of Quality in making a decision about a gift. We consider how we feel and how our friend feels because we have access to the energy of Quality that has been created between the two of us. We know that they will like what we have bought or created because we used our combined energies of Quality as a filter for our reality.

From the moment the invitation arrived to the moment you gave your friend the gift, you were working with transferred energies. This explains why some friends or family members who are very close to one another, know instinctively what the other has planned for them. The excitement that one friend feels can quite possibly be transferred to the other because of the energy they already share. The closer they are in their focus area (heart, eyes, etc.) of Quality, and thus their perception of reality, the more likely they are to pick up on the way the other person feels. If we do not understand and acknowledge this, we may end up ruining the surprise for our friend without uttering a word!

The final transfer of energy in this example, takes place in all matters of anticipation. As everybody waits for your friend to arrive there is a heightened sense of happiness and love, almost always emanating from the area of the heart. (I say "*almost* always" because there may be some people at the party who do not feel the same way about your friend as others. However, it is important to realize that even those who came as guests of someone else and do not know your friend, feel the same pull from their heart area. This is because they are connecting with the feelings of the person with whom they came, and the way *that person* is feeling.) As your friend opens her/his gifts, there is also the same sense of feeling in the heart area. Both of these instances are the result of an energy transfer between our personal sense of Quality and that of the person on whom we are focused.

There is the possibility that some of the people at the party might feel their energy pull from areas other than the heart. This is perfectly normal because as mentioned earlier, each person has Quality energy focused in a different area. However, the majority of people in a situation such as this one, where we assume that most of the guests are happy for the person whose party it is, will connect and transfer energy through the heart. This happens not only because they are picking up energy from others who connect with their hearts, but because they are connecting through the Island of Love.

It is no fallacy that we as a culture assign the definition of "love" with a symbol of the heart. The heart is the center for the Island of Love, and the core from which the energy of love is transferred to others. What we should be aware of however, is that just because this Island takes up residence in the area of the heart, the energy of love is not limited to it. We are capable of using all other parts of our body, and all other sources of energy to transfer the energy we feel within the Island of Love.

Just think for a moment of the times you have looked another person in the eyes to tell them you loved them. The energy of your Island of Love would not allow a lesser action because your sense of Quality demanded the closeness of energies. (I cannot stress the importance of your inner sense of Quality enough. We will always come back to this Island as we pass through the others.)

How would it have felt if the first time someone told you they loved you, they had said it over the telephone? I imagine you would have been disappointed, and the meaning of the words would have probably lost much of their significance. But if the person whom you were fond of cared enough to look deep within themselves to that center of Quality that had entwined with your own, they would certainly have realized that their convictions needed to be expressed in a way that would allow for transference of energy to the fullest extent. The closer two physical bodies are to one another, the stronger the energy that can be transferred between them. Thus, looking another in the eyes as feelings are uttered, makes the event much more potent.

Let us examine the influence of emotions and feelings between a mother and her child while it is still within the womb, and the way that present society chooses to view this, as opposed to what actually happens.

As you probably have read many times, there is evidence in this scientific, show-me-proof world, that what occurs mentally, physically, and emotionally to the mother-to-be, effects the child she carries. Whether we choose to believe this or not, we must assume that the characteristics, physical, emotional, and mental states of the child are the outcome of *something*. We therefore place blame if the child does not live up to what society refers to as "normal". More often than not, the first person to bear the blame is the mother. As a society we are not quite sure why we choose to place blame on the mother. When we take the time to think about this, we usually conclude that since the mother is the one who carried the child within her, and since the child was a part of her, she is the one who is most responsible for the child's state. To think this way—to place blame on someone or something, goes against our inner sense of Love.

Whether you are the mother of a child or not, you can still understand the meaning behind this example. Think of anything that you have created in this lifetime. Have you written an outstanding paper or proposal? Have you painted a magnificent picture, or planted a seed and then nurtured it while it grew into a beautiful flower? How did you feel knowing that what you wrote, what you planted, what you created, was unique because it was filled with the energy you gave it? Imagine the sense of pride you felt when others saw your goal completed.

Take any of these examples and trace the transference of energy from start to completion as we have done in the example of purchasing a gift for a friend. Imagine the energy that began with your idea being added to the energies of the people who manufactured the paper on which you wrote, or the canvas on which you painted. Sometimes we can better understand this transference of energy when we think of something we have tried to do that just wouldn't work for us. We make up all kinds of names for times when the mind is willing, but no other part of us seems capable of producing results ("writer's block", etc.). However, we notice that if we give up and start again another day, or if we change the notebook we were writing in, or the canvas on which we painted, or even the soil in which we planted our flower, our creativity seems to flow. This is all because of the energy level that existed at the time we began our project. Maybe the person who produced our paper at the factory was having a bad day. Perhaps the soil we had been working in had been over-used for many years and needed time to replenish its own energies before it could yield the results we intended. There are endless possibilities as to why things did not turn out the way we planned, but these are not reasons to *blame*. Instead, these are reasons for us to enter our Island of Love and decide what *we* need to change in order to produce what we desire.

Great lessons can be learned from a child who chooses (yes, each of does choose to become a part of this world) to be born with some sort of physical, emotional, or mental handicap. Because the energy that is this child has already mingled with her parents' energies, the child knows what limitations and obstacles will be faced. She knows what kind of problems she will face in this world. The transference of energy that takes place between herself and her parents, allows her to know the risks and the benefits. If the would-be mother smokes or is addicted to drugs, for example, the child knows this. If she will be brought up in a home where one of the parents is abusive, she knows this as well because she can feel it through the energy that emanates around her parent's Island of Love. It is then up to this child to continue with the process of birth, or end it. A miscarriage is a child's way of saying, 'I choose not to be born at this time, because I am not ready to learn the lessons of this particular life'. But we encourage each individual who might have experienced the loss of a child in this manner that if you choose to connect with a would-be child's sense of Love and to become pregnant at another time, you can produce the results you both prefer. Just as picking up a new canvas can lead to a better flow of energy, so the circumstances can be corrected for any soul who chooses to enter this world.

This does not mean that every miscarriage is the result of a child choosing not to be born because it feels its parents' choices have set up a situation into which it cannot exist happily. After all, there are many children who *do* choose to enter into these exact situations. Those who choose to live under such conditions do so for many reasons. But the underlying reason for choosing such an existence, as well as choosing not to be born, even to parents who seemingly did everything right, is a poorly defined Island of Love.

At the beginning of this section, we discussed the release of fear. In order to reap the rewards offered by the Island of Love, each of us must learn to let go of the fears that tie us to things that inhibit our attainment of desires. Perhaps the energy that is the child waiting to be born has had a hard existence on this earth before and does not wish to experience the same things again. This, as well as many other factors, can cause the child understandable apprehension when considering entering this world. Even when these feelings are not justified, the fact that they remain within the energy of the child, shows us that fear is still a big issue. Often the mother-to-be senses this feeling of fear, but attributes it to her own mixed feelings and hormonal changes that take place during her pregnancy. Yet, just as she is capable of sensing the name of her child, (transference of energy that tells her what name would be best based on the energy within the name itself) she is also capable of sensing what the child is feeling. This is the main reason that society tends to blame the mother when things go wrong during the pregnancy and the child is born "lacking". We tend to think at some level that the mother is the one who is greatly in tune with her child and should have known what to do to change the outcome. But often, the mother has done exactly as she should.

Since, in most cases, the mother is so in tune with the workings of her body and the child within, she knows when the energy that is her child is choosing not to be born. The feelings she receives from this energy entwining with hers, let her know that things might not turn out the way she expected. If she is in tune with her own Island of Love, then she has an easier time letting go of the energy that would be her child. This is what the child wants, and she knows this. The Quality of life can be defined only by that energy which chooses to live it. Therefore, if the child's sense of the Quality of life is not one in which they would be happy living, they have the right to try it again at another time. This does not mean that every would-be child is going to decide that a little unhappiness is reason not to be born. In fact, many children are brought into this world knowing that they will face hard times. They have already accepted this because they feel that there are lessons that they need to learn. (This will be discussed further in a future book.) If, on the other hand, the mother senses that the child is afraid to enter the world because of past experiences, being in touch with her Island of Love will enable her to work with the child's energy to help her or him release these fears.

How to Gain Access to the Island of Love

Meditation, combined with visual imagery, is undoubtedly one of the best sources for connecting to your Island of Love. If you are a woman who is currently pregnant, this exercise will work wonderfully for you as well.

Take a few minutes each day to imagine something in your life that makes you feel love within your heart. Close your eyes if necessary, and slowly allow all of the negative or distracting areas of your life to fade away. Hold the feeling of love that you have imagined within your heart, and visualize a strand of it reaching toward your mind (or brain if you think more in the physical sense). When this has been visualized completely, imagine four more strands of energy, one at a time, reaching from your heart to your hands and feet. This five-strand link illustrates the connection we have between our inner and outer being at the five major points by which we first experience the physical world.

Now try to imagine what you desire. What things do you wish to create? What things do you wish to change about yourself? See the energy of love that you have visualized around your heart flowing to those parts of your body that you need to bring into focus in order to acquire your goals. If, for example, you have chosen to paint, see your arms and hands being lifted by the strand of energy that emanates from your heart. See them holding the paintbrush; see them dipping the brush into the vivid hues on your palette. Imagine the canvas in front of you, and see exactly what you wish to create. Notice every brushstroke, and pay attention to every feeling that you may have while you experience this creative visualization. These feelings are the result of energy emanating from the area of your heart, being transferred between you and what you are creating. Because this exercise is designed to get you back in touch with your Island of Love, if you experience anything but happy, energetic feelings you probably need to try again. Begin the visualization process once again from the beginning, but this time instead of seeing yourself in the same position, using the same supplies, change things a little. If you saw yourself in a green meadow, now see yourself by the ocean. If you chose a canvas from a pile, choose one that comes from somewhere else. Change things until you have achieved a state that brings about cheerful feelings. If you are still having trouble by the second try, it is best to put this aside and try again later. (Remember we spoke of sayings such as 'Writer's Block' and the benefits that can be reaped when you put something aside and try again at another time.)

Mothers-to-be can connect with their Islands in the same way we described above, but with a minor variation. After you have envisioned the strands of energy connecting to the five points on *your* body, see them connecting to the same spots on the body *within* you. Once you have established your own energy in these places, imagine the center of the Island of Love within your child. Visualize the strands of energy flowing forth to the places on his or her body (or "bod*ies*", should you be connecting to twins, triplets, etc.) Once you have done this, take the next step and connect your heart energy to theirs, your mind to theirs, your hands, and then your feet. At the moment this is complete, you will feel a wonderful sense of connection. You will know your child/children in a more intimate way than you have up to this point. Each of you will be better able to sense each other's feelings and to interpret them correctly. You might want to continue to make this connection with your child at least once per day, or at special moments such as when you are reading to them, (yes, or course they can hear from within your womb) or enjoying a quiet moment or even a festive party. *Any*time you feel that sharing what you are experiencing with your child will be beneficial, would be an ideal time to take a moment and connect. Once you have done this a few times, it will take you only seconds to reconnect. And these connections do not have to end once the child is born into this world. You can still connect with them in this way. As they get older, you can teach them how to connect with you and those they love in this way as well.

Even if you are not a mother or a mother-to-be, you can practice this exercise with those who are close to you. Once you learn how to connect with other people in this way, you will be amazed at how much clearer your communication and understanding becomes. Choose a person in your life with whom you already share a special bond, and try these exercises together. Pick a special place and go through the steps simultaneously. Some might notice how quickly they connect because they have been connecting at an unconscious level all along. Others may take some time, but it is well worth it for all involved.

Do not worry that these connections will grant others access to a part of you that you do not want them to see. If you are keeping a secret from someone, for example, because you do not wish to hurt their feelings, do not be concerned that they will suddenly know what that secret is. They may sense there is something you are holding back, but the ability to connect with Love lets them know that you are entitled to this. Nobody needs to be told everything because through the Islands within us, we all know what others know. However, we choose to constantly deny this sense of knowing and ask to be shown or told instead, as proof. To reconnect with the Island of Love, or any Island for that matter, gives us the sense of knowing that helps us relate better to others. You might hate what someone has done, or feel terrible because a certain person has betrayed you. But if you had been in touch with your Island of Love all along you would have sensed something was not right, and would have understood the source once you connected your strands of energy to those of the person with whom you had the problem.

How many times have you heard friends or acquaintances, or even yourself saying, "I had a feeling..." The "feeling" to which this person is referring is actually a sense of knowing that creates a feeling within them. Just as the feelings created in our example of the painting were the result of being connected to what we were working with, the "feeling" we had that something was about to happen or that someone was doing something behind our back, came as a result of this same connection. The stronger the feeling, the more connected we are to the person. The more vague the feeling, the less intensely the connection exists.

It is important to note that those individuals who are very fearful, as well as those who exhibit such emotions as suspicion, defensiveness, or jealousy, to name a few, have poorly developed Islands of Love. When they allow the world to witness these emotions they are indeed telling us they have forgotten how to connect to others. Instead of trying to reestablish these connections, they prefer to attempt to sever them in others. They do not realize that they have the ability to change what is within themselves, so they try to change others. By keeping others from connecting to their own Islands, they establish a safety zone for themselves. If a person cannot connect to what is inside of themselves, they cannot properly connect to what exists within others. Therefore, someone who is suspicious and jealous feels better momentarily if they can keep others from connecting with them. These feelings are all they have, and although they may not make the person feel particularly happy, they get around this by making sure that others do not attempt to understand them. If someone were to make the connection with a person who was jealous or suspicious, (although it would be hard because this person is not willing to meet half way and share their energies willingly) they would be given insight into the realm from which the feelings stemmed. (Most often they originate from a sense of fear.) The person with these feelings often cannot allow this, because it would shatter the world they were trying to create; a world where they placed the blame for their feelings on others.

If you examine someone who has the type of life we have just described, you will better understand what we mean. Picture someone you know, or have known, who was very jealous, suspicious, pessimistic, etc. Inevitably, there is at least one person who is very close to them, on whom they have chosen to place the blame for their feelings. If this person is not in touch with their own Island of Love, they will start to believe that they truly are to blame, and will do all they can to change the situation so that the other person feels better. As many of us know, this does not work. The person who is not happy remains that way because there is no incentive for them to change. They have convinced the person they placed blame upon that *he* or *she* is the one who needs to change, and so that person believes it. (We see this many times in situations of emotional or physical abuse.) If the person who bears the blame were to reach within themselves and reconnect with their Island of Love, they would understand that their actions cannot bring about the true happiness that the other desires. Nothing but a false sense of happiness can come from forcing others to disconnect from loving themselves. When this is allowed to happen, we cannot see the Island of Love through the fog we created. To allow someone else to take hold of our feelings and force us to sacrifice in order to bring them a happiness that cannot exist under the terms that they established, is just one example of what can happen if we do not reconnect with the next Island; the Island of Knowledge.

THE ISLAND
OF
KNOWLEDGE

Sometimes the winds carry old, familiar smells.
Pete

Once you have revisited and recognized your true sense of Quality and learned to release the fears that hold you back from connecting to the Island of Love, you are ready to approach the Island of Knowledge.

The Island of Knowledge is, like the previous Islands we visited, based upon our personal Truths. When we visit this Island we do not automatically become the recipients of all the vast knowledge that exists in the universe. Just as you make the choice to visit the library when you need to expand and learn, you must make the choice to visit your personal Island and draw from it the information you need.

As we had mentioned in the previous section, (Island of Love) allowing one's self to be cut off from the Islands within, creates great unhappiness. When we learn to reconnect, we learn that we do not have to be satisfied with this state of unhappiness. Because we are all connected through our Islands, we can all draw from their resources to discover where true happiness lies. Let us look at an example of this.

Suppose you are in the type of relationship described under the Island of Love. Assume your partner has acted in such a way that you chose (consciously or unconsciously) to sacrifice your happiness in the hope that your partner would be happy. Weeks, months, or even years later, you finally realize that what you have done, although you thought it was a loving act at the time, has not only *not* made your partner any happier, but has in fact made *you* so unhappy that you do not know how you can change things. If you had been in touch with your Island of Knowledge before you chose to make a decision that resulted in your unhappiness, you would have not chosen as you did. This is because within our Island of Knowledge, we have access to resources that help us examine the actions and thoughts of those who came before us. All past discoveries lie within the sands of this Island, and it only takes the ability to reconnect to it to gain access to the information it offers.

Had you been the person in the situation we just described, but with access to your Island of Knowledge, you would have been able to pull the correct book from the library of the universe. In it, you would have found the reasons you were considering choosing as you did, based upon the experiences of others who had chosen the same or similar pathways. The transfer of energies between your Island of Knowledge and the Islands of others, would have placed you in a position to know what the outcome of your decision would have been.

Unfortunately, when we choose not to acknowledge the energy that flows to us through our Islands from others, we are destined to repeat mistakes and remain stagnant. We can take great leaps forward in our existence if we choose to open to the Universe and learn from the mistakes of others. Of course we all do make mistakes. This is part of our learning process that leads to our eventual advancement. But just think of how much faster we all could advance if we learned to tap into the center of our Knowledge that also extends to others. Some of the mistakes that we may feel we are destined to make can be avoided if we open the correct book and read what others have written.

Do not confuse what happens on the Island of Knowledge with what others may have told you in your lifetime. Allowing someone else to attempt to teach you with such statements as, "I'm doing this for your own good," is not the same as you tapping into the energy on your own. A situation where someone tries to hurt you, or tries to cause a negative reaction in order to get their point across, is different because they are attempting to force you into thinking the knowledge that *they* have gained is exactly what *you* need. The fact is, they may not have learned the lesson they were meant to master and instead of *helping* you they are actually passing their mistakes along to you. This process, the pathway of lessons not learned, is what many refer to as "Karma".

Even though the concept of Karma exists within our energy pool to various extents, it does not have control over us. We perpetuate the existence of Karma when we make choices that we understand will cause a specific outcome. When we receive the outcome we wished for, Karma is often the least likely word we would choose to describe our result. However, when something happens that we consider negative or less desirable, we reach for such explanations as Karma; the law of cause and effect. Once again, we have chosen to rely on a source outside of ourselves to place blame upon. Because we are not always in tune with the energies within and around us, we tend to imagine that some force exists outside ourselves that causes things to happen. Our Island of Knowledge tells us differently, however. While reconnecting with our Island of Knowledge, we come to understand that Karma is not simply a matter of cause and effect, but what we experience as a direct result of the lessons we choose *not* to learn.

It is important for you to understand that although we all establish connections to one another through the energies of our Islands, the connections are not there to force us to act out a particular situation in order to learn from it. We may have already acted out the situation we are facing in a previous existence. (We say "previous" here as a direct referral to your understanding of time.) To understand this better, take a few moments to imagine a part of history that you feel particularly drawn to. Can you picture yourself walking under the Wisteria of a Southern plantation? Or fighting with sword and shield outside castle walls? There are endless possibilities to the time periods to which you may be drawn. Sometimes they do not manifest in your memory as an entire scene, but you catch glimpses of them when you pass certain objects or read certain books. You may also notice a strong feeling toward a particular style of clothing, a type of house, or ethnic music. All of these experiences are either hints of existences you have lived, or existences that the energies you have drawn to yourself have encountered. Whether you have actually lived these lives yourself, or have tapped into the experiences of other energies/souls, the time periods to which you are drawn become your personal history. They assist you in gathering information that can be a great benefit for your present lifetime because within these energies are the clues to your personal Truth. Look to these energies as guides, assistants, even friends, for contained within each one of their lives, as well as your own, are many lessons. If, during a particular existence we chose not to learn one of these lessons, or we do not listen to the energies that can help us, we will be confronted with the lesson at another time. Remember, this is a choice that we make, and the choice to put things off and learn from them later is perfectly acceptable. At this point, we believe an example is in order.

Suppose you are involved in a relationship in which you feel threatened. This can be a relationship with your partner, a relationship with a co-worker or boss, or a relationship with just about anyone. Perhaps this person is not threatening you in a physical way, but they are "holding something over your head," shall we say. The very idea that you have allowed yourself to feel threatened by this person shows us two things. The first is that you believe deep within yourself you must experience this type of treatment in order to learn from it. The second points to your belief that you can become "a better person" by changing yourself in such a way that the other person's treatment of you changes as well. You have slipped so far away from your Island of Knowledge that you no longer understand you do *not* have to experience this relationship fully in order to learn the lessons it was meant to teach.

You think that there is a reason you are in this type of relationship. Perhaps you fear letting go of it because you might be destined to repeat it at another time, or in another existence. If this is what you have chosen, then yes, you will be confronted by this relationship at another time. But if you learn to tap into your Island of Knowledge and "read" the outcome of your previous experiences, you will not have to repeat the relationship on the physical level. Allow us to use the previous comparison between the Island of Knowledge and a library, to further illustrate this point.

Imagine yourself in a classroom. Your teacher has just assigned a project dealing with a subject you know very little about. In order to find the information you need to begin your work, you make a conscious decision to visit your local library. Before you reach the library, you already know the steps you must take in order to retrieve the information you desire. You may not know *exactly* what you will learn from your experience, but you can imagine what is necessary to get you to that point. You see the doors that you must pass through in order to enter the library. You see the card catalog or computer from which you will be guided to the correct books in the library. And you see yourself moving to each of these places until you reach the shelf on which the information you need lies. All that is left for you to do is grasp the correct book(s) and read the contents.

You may notice that some of the information contained within the book(s) you chose becomes Truth to you. For example, you might not have visited the Great Pyramids in Egypt, but you accept that they exist based upon the words and the photos that describe them. At other points in the book(s) however, you read information that does not seem true to you. Maybe you choose not to accept the theory that the Pyramids were built by beings from another universe. These decisions are based largely on what you have experienced in the past. Considering that you had no previous conscious knowledge of the Pyramids before you began you work, reveals that you tapped into the energy of the Island of Knowledge in order to develop these basic Truths. What you chose to accept and what you chose to reject are items that you have either experienced in past lives, or items that others have experienced and are now sharing with you through a transference of energies. Since we all have the ability to tap into this vast library of experience, the final decision in the matter of personal choice, and therefore our definition of reality, comes only after we filter it through the Island of Quality.

If we apply what we have learned with the help of this illustration, we come to understand that in order to open the doors to our own library, our Island of Knowledge, all we have to do is believe it is possible. We already know where the "card catalog" exists, we just need to direct ourselves to the right "book".

How to Gain Access to the Island of Knowledge

Once again, we contend that visual imagery is a very good source for reconnecting with the Island of Knowledge. But this is not the only source. Because the success of your visualization depends mainly upon your ability to see the library that was described at the beginning of this section, you can "cheat" a little and ensure success by actually visiting a physical library. Some people find they are better able to create the imagery they need if they find a quiet place in the library and work from there. Being surrounded by a physical library often helps some to not have to work as hard trying to imagine this part of the exercise. But since each person's creativity varies, this part is entirely up to you.

Whether you opt for a trip to the library, or decide to visualize your library from another place, be sure to make yourself aware of the details associated with your library of choice. The way a person imagines their library is just as important as the physical library that another person chooses to visit. For example, if you imagine or visit a library that is very old, you can be assured you are preparing yourself to work with the past. Your Island of Knowledge will be accessed through the history and previous lives you have experienced prior to this one. On the other hand, if your library of choice is a more modern building you will find that your Island of Knowledge surfaces with the help of more recent experiences. These principles are not only true for the libraries we imagine. Those people who choose to visit a physical library make the decision, consciously and unconsciously to some degree, to find a library in which they feel most comfortable. They will not go to their local library unless they feel it is the one in which they need to work. There are, after all, many other libraries for them to visit, and the one they finally choose indicates what they will be working with in order to reach their Island of Knowledge.

After you have studied the building itself to determine the area in which you will be working, picture yourself in (or enter, if you are there physically) the library. Pay attention to all the details once again. Observe how much sunlight flows through the windows of the library. If there is an abundance of light, you can assume you have chosen to be enlightened. Therefore, reconnecting to your Island of Knowledge will not be hard for you. If however, there is very little or no sunlight in the area, try to visualize yourself moving throughout the library until you find a place that offers more. The less light you allow yourself to see and feel, the harder it will be for you to reconnect. This lack of sunlight is a symbol that your mind has created. You use it as a way of telling yourself you are frightened of what you might find on your Island, as well as a way of convincing yourself you do not want the responsibility of being enlightened. But as you go through your library, try to remember the only thing you have to fear is allowing yourself *not* to be enlightened. If you have come this far, it is because the Truth within you is calling out for recognition. And the only way for you to recognize it, is to reconnect with it.

As you explore your library, take note not only of the details, but any feelings you may have as a result of your visitation. Examine all parts of the library and formulate questions about each of them. You might ask yourself what feeling you get from the people who are in the library. Are they friendly or do they seem annoyed by your presence? Or perhaps you have chosen not to encounter any people while you are visiting the library. Perhaps it is dark and after regular hours. If this is the case, substitute moonlight for sunlight in the example we used earlier, but know that moonlight means you are preparing to be enlightened in a way that leads toward an understanding of the so-called mysterious realms of existence. In other words, you will gain Knowledge in areas that are spiritual, or as some prefer to call it, "other-worldly."

Take time to truly understand the feelings that develop during your visit. Determine why you feel a certain way toward the different things that you encounter. There are no right or wrong answers to what you are experiencing. The fact that some people may encounter friendly librarians, and others may not, does not mean that you must strive to change whatever it is you meet. Just know that you are encountering these personalities for a reason. For example, a friendly librarian is a creation that can help you find the books, or Knowledge you need. A librarian who is not very friendly will cause you to ask yourself why you have created this blockage within yourself. Because you have the answers to things such as this in your Island of Knowledge, attempt to connect with this librarian and ask why there appears to be a problem. See a beautiful island with glowing sand, growing larger and larger until it reaches the librarian. Imagine yourself walking across the island to meet her/him, and then ask them if they could help you. The friendly librarian will most certainly help you in anyway possible. The unfriendly librarian however, will let you know why they act as they do. This may take several attempts until you finally have your answers, so do not despair. You may be so out of touch with your Island of Knowledge that it will take you a little longer to establish contact. Once you know why you have chosen to bring this personality into your library, you will understand what you need to do to hurdle this blockage.

When you have established contact with any personalities in your library that you choose to, you are ready to move on to the part of the library that holds shelves of books. (Some of you may choose not to visit a library that contains shelves, and this is all right, too. Remember, what you visualize is entirely up to you.) Begin at the end of each aisle, each set of steps, or whatever you have created as the organizing factor for your books. (If you are the type who finds order in disorder, you can visualize this too.) Take the time to pause long enough at the end of each row, etc. to notice which section you are in. After you have established the section, (Fiction, Non-Fiction, Biography, etc.) pay particular attention to any feelings that you have. Do you experience feelings of fright when you visit this section, or do you fill with anticipatory happiness? If you feel neutral toward this section, move onto the next. Feelings of neutrality indicate that you have not experienced the lessons of this section, either firsthand or through others, and do not need to dwell. However, remember how you came to this section in case you need to tap into its wealth of information sometime in the future.

If you notice you are experiencing fright in a particular section, take note of that section and then narrow it down. If you do not feel comfortable enough with what you might discover, you can skip these aisles and return to them at another time when you might need the knowledge they offer. If you choose to continue, proceed down the aisle (we will continue to use "aisle" for our example, though you may choose to substitute any word you wish) until you see the section that causes you to feel fearful. Choose a book from the shelf in this section, and look at the title. Does it indicate a place, a time period, or a particular person? Maybe the title is a single word. Whatever the words or picture on the book describe, you can be certain is the cause of your feeling(s). You have either encountered a frightful experience within this area, or you are connected with the energy of someone who has. Because you have lived many times and in many places in an attempt to learn valuable lessons, it is not hard for you to imagine that some of your past experiences may still be held within the energy that is in and around you. Perhaps you did not learn all that you could have, and are about to repeat the choices that lead you in this direction before. Having the ability to tap into your Island of Knowledge allows you to understand which circumstances lead you to experience this fright, and the choices you now have to change and learn from them.

If you are not the person who experienced the fright originally, you will know this by looking closely at the book you hold. Look at the name of the author. Is it you or someone else? If it is indeed someone else, realize you have tapped into another's energy because you are now ready to learn from their choices. Let's say that they were involved in a fatal accident caused by another person. If this is the same situation you are facing with someone in your life, you have tapped into their energy as a way to help you choose a different path. Since you always have the chance to make choices in your existence you can choose to continue on the path you have set so far, or you can make the choice to change your direction based upon your newly acquired Knowledge.

For those who reach the end of an aisle and discover that they feel happily drawn to investigate it further, you must know you are in for a good experience. Most likely you are recalling a wonderful time in your many existences, and all of the necessary things should be noted. In what section do you find yourself? To what area within this section are you drawn? What is the title or picture on the book? Who is the author? As in the example above, these are all things to consider for further enlightenment.

Too often, society presses us to believe that the negative elements that surface in our lives are the ones we must pay attention to and learn from. But when things happen that make us experience happiness, we often fail to see the lessons in them. It is important to remember that at all levels the energy that is in and around each of us, is striving for happiness. The wonderful feelings we experience as a result of the good things that enter our lives, are all bits of a map that can lead us toward a fulfilling and happy state if we choose to follow them. So while you are journeying through your library, pay as much attention to the happy moments as you do to the unhappy ones. To reconnect with each of these offers you the chance to delve within them and then release them. Releasing does not imply forgetting, however. To truly release these feelings means that you choose to transfer energy so that it may be useful to others. Just as others have chosen to allow you access to their Knowledge, (what you find within your library) you can allow others access to yours. This is all done via a simple process while you are still within your library.

If you have experienced happiness that you feel others would benefit from, create a book. The same is true for any feelings that you do not like. Others who choose to tap into their own Islands of Knowledge may be going through a situation which is similar to the one you experienced. Even if you did not learn all that you could from the experience, the Knowledge that you did acquire will inevitably help someone else to learn more than they would have, had they not been in touch with their Island. By creating "books", you not only help others discover happiness, but you help yourself as well.

If you have left your library, imagine yourself within its walls once more. Find a section that appears to be empty and make this section your own. Visualize many books on the shelves, all of which are blank at the moment. Decide which experiences you want to create books for, and pull that many books off the shelves. Create all the details of the books. Imagine the colors of the books, the pictures, (if there are any) the words of the title, etc. In other words, create your book any way that you feel would be of benefit to those who find it and read it. As you do this, realize that you are transferring energy. The thoughts and feelings you had in connection to the occurrence you are now creating a book for, are being poured into that book. When you have finished, place the book back on a shelf and walk back to the end of the aisle. Give your section a heading, and you are done. There is no longer a need for you to dwell on these feelings because you have so much more to learn. Yet they will continue to exist to help others, and to help you whenever you feel you must reconnect to them in order to learn something further. If you prefer, you can keep a journal to record the lessons and experiences you have revisited, as well as the books you have created and their various sections. This will enable you to find them quickly during future visits to your library, thus making the Island of Knowledge easier for you to reach.

Once you have finished exploring your library, you are free to leave it in any way that you wish. If you saw yourself as the librarian, perhaps you leave by locking the door. If you crept into the library in the middle of the night, perhaps you prefer to jump from the roof into a tall tree. However you choose to leave this Island, try to make it fun. You have tapped into a vital resource that should leave you with a sense of happiness as you move away from it. To allow this happiness to extend to your choice of exit would be to your benefit, since a pathway created by happiness will enable you to feel good about future visitations.

As you carry the experience of these energies with you, let us move onto our next Island; the Island of Beauty.

The Island

of

Beauty

The gardens of the mind are beautiful indeed.
Pete

Of all the Islands mentioned thus far, it is the Island of Beauty that we glimpse most often. Those who believe in past-lives are most often in touch with the Island of Beauty. (It is important to point out that we all have experienced "past-lives" at some level, though the definition may be different in our separate views of reality. This is a topic that will be explored in depth at another time; perhaps in another book.) Even those who do not believe in past-lives per se, experience the feelings that connect us to this Island.

In the society in which you live, you often hear sayings such as, "Beauty is in the eye of the beholder." Statements such as this one are understood to mean that our value of Beauty resides within each of us as individuals. In turn, we each derive our sense of Beauty from our unique view of Quality. But where did we develop our unique sense of Quality, which acts as the foundation for our judge of Beauty? In order to find this answer we must be willing to look to that part of our memory which includes our previous existences. For those who do not define their experiences in such a way, you may choose to refer to these as moments of "deja-vous".

Think of the moments in your life when you have experienced a sense of "knowing". In other words, think of the times when you have passed a particular place or detected a particular scent, and became vaguely aware that you had experienced this before in conjunction with an event that had since lapsed from your memory. Be aware however, that even though the event might have slipped from your conscious mind, you have not forgotten it entirely. Enough fragments remain for you to recognize that there is a connection, though your mind may not be entirely aware of the origins of that connection. Your mind does not always tell you all you need to know. As we have discussed in previous sections, our Truths can appear to emanate from different parts of our physical bodies. To understand this better, we offer a few examples.

Suppose as a young person you spent many summers at your grandparents' house. You had a great deal of fun during these summers, and have very fond memories of your visits there. Your grandparents' house was an older house with an open front porch, on which you and they would spend the evenings talking and laughing together. To one side of the porch there was a lilac bush that sent its pungent fragrance into the air. Even though you might not have paid close attention to the lilac bush as a child, a part of you did notice that it was there and connected it to the happy times you shared with your grandparents. The best way to determine which part of you was deeply touched by this memory, is to imagine the feelings you get when you detect the scent of lilacs now. Do all of the memories of your grandparents come flooding back to your mind? Or do you feel an overwhelming surge of emotion within your heart? Of course, there are other places within and on the physical body where you can experience sensations like the one we just described. If, for example, your grandparents had a rose bush instead of a lilac bush and you had fallen into it at some point and been badly scratched by the thorns, you might experience feelings of pain associated with the smell of roses. Often, a situation such as this is the case when we are confronted with mixed emotions concerning an event that took place within our present lifetime. We are reminded of something wonderful by a scent, a scene, etc., yet we feel pain or sorrow and do not quite understand why. At these moments it is best to get in touch with our Island of Beauty (demonstrated later in this section) and investigate the cause. By doing so, we are not only able to understand why we feel as we do, but we come to a better understanding of the place from which our sense of Beauty arrives.

If you had an experience like the one mentioned in association with the lilac bush, then you already know why you find Beauty in the scent of the flower. The pleasant energies that you associated with your visits mingled with the lilac's fragrance, as well as many other scents, scenes, textures, etc. If, on the other hand, you were the individual who happened to fall into the rose bush at a young age, but over the years have forgotten about this event, getting back in touch with your Island of Beauty will help you to understand why you have an aversion to the smell of roses, and do not recognize the Beauty within them. An event such as this one could also have been the reason you developed an allergy to roses. Yes, manifestations such as allergies do exist in the physical body many times because of an event that happened in the past. More often than not however, the cause results from a previous existence, and the allergy is a hint of something we still must learn. To understand how this can happen, let us turn our attention to animals.

Suppose you are a person who is very allergic to cats. Whether other members of your physical family are allergic to cats or not, sometimes has no bearing on why *you* became allergic. We will go back to something that has been enforced many times throughout this book… Because you have, and have always had freedom of choice, the circumstances you chose lead up to your allergy. This does not mean that the choices you made had to be made within your present lifetime, however. Many people develop allergies in this existence because of a choice they made in a previous one.

In another existence you may have made the choice to destroy cats. Perhaps you lived in a country that suffered a terrible famine. There had always been a plethora of stray cats in your area and now that the famine has occurred, they are competing with people and other animals for scraps of food and milk. You do not dislike cats. In fact, you have always been able to recognize the Beauty within them, and have always treated them as living things should be treated (with kindness). But since the famine appears to be getting worse, you realize that you must make a decision regarding the way you treat these cats. After careful thought, you decide that killing the cats is your only alternative. Others have already begun this practice, so you convince yourself this is what you should be doing as well. But deep within you, you know this is wrong. You feel horrible about what you are doing, but you justify it somehow and continue to do it. Because you have made a decision that goes against your inner Truth, you have set yourself up for manifestations such as allergies to occur in other existences.

Whenever you make a decision to violate your inner Truth, you put yourself in a position to have to relearn that lesson. In the situation mentioned above, you had already learned to be kind to cats. By going against your inner sense of Truth, you chose to deny this lesson. We are not saying you were wrong for making the choice that you did. No one can decide what is "right" and "wrong" except you, because this insight comes from your own sense of Truth. Since each of us has a different set of criteria for our Truths, none of us can be in the position to judge for another. Therefore the lesson that must be re-learned before your allergies can subside, is the particular act that *you* (as the person in the example) had committed that defied your personal sense of Truth .

Even if you enter your present existence with the idea that you are going to be kind to all animals, if you did not come to peace with the choice you made in your previous existence, hints of what you chose to do will surface. Sometimes allergies occur; sometimes you feel an overwhelming sense of sadness when you see a cat. Again, there are infinite possibilities to how this can manifest. But no matter how they do reveal themselves, you should recognize that they are there to force you to acknowledge that you have some lesson to learn or re-learn. You have created them yourself in an effort to recapture the Beauty that you once felt for all things, and will eventually come to feel again once you have reconnected with your Island of Beauty.

If you are not completely in touch with your Island of Beauty, you will often find yourself perplexed by the great differences in opinions in your society. If, for example, you think a particular painting is "awful" or "ugly", and cannot see an ounce of Beauty in it, you will find it hard to believe that another person would be able to view the same painting and call it "lovely" or "beautiful". But what we all must understand is that these differences in opinion stem from how in-touch we are with our Island of Beauty.

Pretend that you and a close friend are observing some paintings in a museum or gallery. You come to a painting that contains one red circle on a white background. Other than that circle, there is nothing else visible on the white background. You think the painting cannot be considered art because it required very little talent to create it. The phrase that most often comes to mind is, "Anyone could have done that!" But your friend sees the painting differently. Because your friend is in touch with their Island of Beauty, they can see beyond the circle on the white background. They form images in their mind based upon what they see, and begin to relate these images to the painting. Their inner sense of Beauty tells them that a red circle can be seen in the setting sun, or a beach ball that in turn reminds them of a wonderful day at the shore. They can see the white background as symbolic of innocence and purity, and the red circle as the next step toward maturity. No matter how they view the painting they are ultimately drawing from that place within themselves that conjures memories (of their present lifetime, or others) that had a lasting emotional effect on them. They are not stuck in the present moment only, and therefore are not limited to what they see. They see the painting as beautiful because it has acted as the catalyst that brought memories of Beauty to the surface for them. For those who see the red circle on the white background and do not know how to allow their memories of Beauty to surface, the painting will continue to appear less than beautiful.

Even the artist who created the painting was aware at some level that her/his image would inspire forgotten memories and stir up new ones in those who connected to their personal Islands. Since everyone's sense of

Quality is different, there is certainly no way the artist could have pre-dicted what *type* of memories these would be, or which new thoughts their painting would inspire. However, they *were* aware of the power within their creation, just as we are all aware of the power within ourselves each time we reconnect with another Island.

How to Gain Access to the Island of Beauty

Getting back in touch with your Island of Beauty requires that you become aware of the things that you have drawn into your life. As this society often phrases this, "What do you identify with?"

The first step to figuring out what we each "identify with", is to raise our level of awareness on the subject. As the previous re-connecting exercises explained, meditation is a very important part of reaching our Islands. But before we begin any form of meditation, we each need to clarify the parts of our lives where we find Beauty.

When you find that you have some quiet time to yourself, write down the things in your life that you recognize for their Beauty. These can be material things or non-material things. They can also consist of things that are part of your everyday life, such as your style of clothing, or the sunset that you witness everyday on your ride home from work. Scenes that you do not witness everyday, like the view from your favorite vacation spot, are also items of Beauty that can be included. Do not think you should be able to write down everything that is beautiful in your life in one session. Feel free to carry the list with you for weeks or months, or however long it takes to comprise your Beauty register. While your list is under construction, also be aware of the things in your life that you do not find beautiful and make a list of those as well.

Once your lists are complete, (or as close to complete as you feel necessary to move on to the next step) begin to ask yourself questions pertaining to each item. Ask yourself why you find certain items beautiful while other items are less than beautiful, or even ugly to you. Sometimes you do not have to go into a meditative state in order to access this information. There are many answers that you will understand on a conscious level if you force yourself to stay with the subject until your mind acknowledges it. For example, you might have listed a co-worker's tie under "ugly", but never really questioned why you felt the way you did about it. You never tried to understand why the tie offended you, but preferred to live with the feelings of ugliness that you felt every time this co-worker wore this particular tie. If you took the time to question your feelings however, you might discover that the tie reminds you of one that a previous boss, who belittled you, used to wear.

The way that we come to understand this, is by capturing the feeling that we experience each time we see the tie and searching for its source within us. If we feel anger or sadness within the area of our heart, we know the tie is reminding us of an experience involving love. If we experience feelings that emanate from the area of our head, we know the problem stems from something connected with the mind or intellect. (See examples under Getting In Touch With Your Island of Quality.) In the case of the tie, the fact that a boss belittled you even though you and he were of equal intelligence and related to one another in this way, the feelings you experienced would manifest around the area of the head (thought) or throat (verbal communication). If there were other ways in which you and your previous boss related, then your feelings would point you toward other areas of the physical body and the energies existing in and around those areas.

Once again we must access our Island of Quality in order to better understand the Island of Beauty. Our sense of Quality helps us define what is beautiful, or not beautiful, and also works with our Island of Beauty to let us know why we feel the way we do. The difference between the feelings and energies associated with our Island of Quality and our Island of Beauty lies in our connected-ness.

As we had mentioned in our section on Quality, often we find ourselves thinking of redecorating or changing clothing styles because we are connected to the energies of the Islands of others, and the time has come for an alteration in our reality. But when we reach the Island of Beauty, we discover a different type of connected-ness. This one does not spring from a connection to many other individuals and their Islands, but from an experience we have had with *one other person*. The example of your reaction toward your co-worker's tie will help you understand this message more clearly. The fact that you disliked this person's tie was not because you were connecting with the Islands of Quality throughout your office, but because you had had a personal experience involving a similar tie. You had defined your sense of Beauty based upon an unhappy experience that *you* had had. Others in your office might have actually liked your previous boss, and therefore will not have the same reaction to the tie as you did. There is no change needed in the overall scheme of things, so Quality would not be the forerunner here. There is change needed on a more personal level however, as you still have not learned how to let go of the unhappy memories associated with your previous boss and the tie that reminds you of her/him. Because the area that you are dealing with is more individualistic, the Island of Beauty takes front stage.

It is through our Island of Beauty that we draw from the past in order to find a more pleasing view of the future. If we know why we feel the way we do about the things that we find beautiful, we can choose to continue to bring those energies into our lives and continue to enjoy the happiness that they allow us to experience. If, on the other hand, we choose to hang onto the feelings of unhappiness associated with the sense of ugliness brought on by our past experiences, we will never effectively recognize the Beauty inherent in all things. Once the unhappiness and the ugliness is acknowledged, we can learn to separate it from the object or image that we associate it with, and let it go. If we understand it is not the object (in our example, the tie) that causes our feelings, we can begin to notice the Beauty in the tie itself. By concentrating on each item on our list, one at a time, we will re-learn how to see our Truth in the area of Beauty.

If you have tried to understand the reasons you feel the way you do about the items on your lists and still have not been able to comprehend why you perceive them as you do, you may need to begin the meditative process.

Begin by finding a quiet place and relaxing. (If you need the aid of a med-itative cassette or CD, or even just relaxing music, feel free to use these at any time.) Clear your mind of the day's clutter, and concentrate on one of the items on your list. (You will probably have several items that you need to pay attention to, but it is best to work with them one at a time.)

Go through the initial step mentioned earlier in this section, and ask yourself questions that help you examine *why* you feel the way you do toward the item on your list. (Remember you are not limited to "bad" or "negative" feelings. You can gain better insight into your reasons for find-ing Beauty in your world by meditating on the things you already find beautiful.) If you sense you are blocking the information from surfacing, try to feel where within your physical body you have positioned this blockage. If it is in the area of your heart, for example, imagine the energy that is in and around your heart connecting to the object on your list. As strange as this might sound at first, because after all you are working with an object in most cases and not a person, begin to imagine yourself estab-lishing a relationship with the object. See yourself touching the object, tasting the object, or smelling the object. What feelings are you forming based on these connections? From what part of your physical body do these feelings emanate? And most importantly, what other images appear as you concentrate on this particular item?

Sometimes the feelings that form once you have made a deeper connec-tion with the object, answer the questions for which you seek clarity. After all, you had initially made a connection to this object when the original event occurred. Whether you were consciously aware of it or not, you placed enough energies within and around the object that you perceived as a definite part of the event, (or person, etc.) that you became connected to it. In the episode mentioned earlier about the tie, you experienced a trans-ference of energy when you took your feelings toward your boss and placed them in an item he wore. You then experienced this transference once again when you noticed the tie on a co-worker and were reminded of the feelings you had previously. The energy went from your boss, to you, to his tie, only to be temporarily forgotten once your boss was out of the picture. When you came into contact with a similar tie, energy was stimulated from within you, and your sense of Beauty put a negative label on it.

There are other times when your questions are not so readily answered, and you must rely upon other images that you receive during your meditation for the Truth behind your feelings.

As you concentrate on the item you wish to learn more about, be sure to pay attention not only to your feelings, but to the images that appear in your mind's eye. Very often you will encounter images that remind you of the original event from which you are attempting to gain answers. This process works in a similar way to the "stream-of-consciousness" that many writers find helpful in narrowing a subject for their work. Since all things are connected by varying degrees of energy, it makes sense that your energies would be stirred most profoundly by those which are the strongest. If we use the example of the tie, we can see that the emotional effect it had on you, is the strongest source of energy. In order to better understand the event which transpired to make you feel as you do, you need to start with this source. By tapping into this energy first, you create a wave of power that flows from this source on a path toward the answers you seek. This energy is valuable because it mends broken or temporarily forgotten pathways, and allows each of us to tap into the smaller aspects of the puzzle by lending the energy needed to bring them to the surface. Since we have used the example of the tie so often, we will continue using it to further demonstrate this principle.

As you are meditating in your quest to find the source of your unhappiness concerning your co-worker's tie, allow yourself to feel the power *within* your feelings. Stay with the feelings that arise as a result of imagining the tie. Do not attempt to push them out of your mind, or any other source from which they seem to enter. Hold onto the feeling(s) and feel it as deeply as you possibly can. When you feel it as strongly as you feel you are able to, know that you have succeeded in tapping into your source of power in this matter. Take that acknowledged sense of power and link it to all of the sensations and images that you are now experiencing. You should begin to "see" pieces of the total experience, from which you can form conclusions, and ultimately produce the answers you are seeking. If you are concentrating on the tie, you might "see" a different suit than the one that your co-worker wore with his tie. Or you might "see" the image of blond hair when you know that your co-worker's hair is brown. Once you have gathered as many images as you need, you can start putting them together to form one final image. Usually by the third or fourth image, you are almost positive of your answer, or in this case, the person in question. Do not be discouraged however, if the final image takes you a few tries to uncover. Many times we are afraid to allow our source of energy to uncover the answers that a part of seeks. But if we let go of the fear that we have, and allow our energy to open pathways for us, we will not be disappointed by what we find.

Know that the energy that is in and around you constantly seeks the Truth of each inner Island. And without this Truth, we cannot be as happy as we are meant to be. Here, in the Island of Beauty, we can begin our search for Truth only if we learn why it is that we can see the Beauty in some things and not others. Once this realization is ours, the power to let go of fear and open to the Beauty in all things emerges. And this power takes us to our next Island; the Island of Balance.

The Island
of
Balance

Not learning is the only trap.
Pete and Mejik

As we step away from the Island of Beauty, we carry with us the sense of our inner Truth that comes as a result of recognition. This wonderful sense of power is but a glimpse of the happiness that awaits us when we understand the lessons of the Island of Balance.

Through the Island of Beauty, you were able to identify those things that qualified as beautiful, as well as those things that you found lacking. By understanding why you classified things as you did, you were able to create a path within yourself that lead further toward your sense of Truth. Having reached the Island of Balance, we prepare to bring that Truth into the world in which you exist, thus creating equilibrium between what exists within you, and what exists around you.

Pause for a moment to look around you. Wherever you are, whatever you are doing, take some time to examine the environment in which you currently exist. At this point, you should be working with all of your senses and should take note of the things around you through many different avenues. You may begin by working with your sense of vision, or the imagery that you conjure when your eyes are closed. You may also choose to examine your environment through your sense of smell or touch. However you begin your examination is up to you, but you should ask yourself certain questions, and be prepared to stay with that question until you have an answer. For example, let us imagine that you are outside of a building. You first notice how bright the sun is shining because it hurts your eyes. If you are sensitive to sunlight, you might even notice that it causes you to sneeze, thus touching upon the area associated with your sense of smell. But do not assume that these are the only reasons you have noticed the intensity of the light. You may see the brightness, you might have felt the slight pain that forced your eyes to squint, or you might have sneezed, but the question you must ask yourself as you visit this Island is, "Why?" Why have you noticed the intensity of the sunlight today? Whether you focus on your sight or other senses in this example, you must go beyond these to seek your answer.

The fact that you noticed the brightness of the sun this day, arises from recent encounters you have had with its complement. (You may prefer the use of the word "opposite" here.) In other words, the experiences you have had in times that were not sunny, such as the nighttime, or rainy, cloudy days. Perhaps the reason you noticed the intensity of the sunlight on this particular day, is because it has been raining for the last few days, creating a gray sky that has not allowed much sunlight through. Or perhaps you have just awakened and emerged from your home after your part of the world has experienced the dark of the night. These are only two possibilities, and of course many more exist. But the reason you notice the sunlight at all, is because you are aware of those times when there is little or no sunlight.

None of us can be fully aware of anything without being aware that there exists an opposite or complement to that thing. You would not know how to define light if you did not have the dark to compare it to, thus enabling yourself to create a distinction. One cannot exist independent of the other since each relies on the other for Balance. Without dark, there would be no reason to recognize or appreciate light, since we would have only one element that would remain constant. But since this is not the way we have chosen to live this existence, we must understand the way Balance is applied.

One of the best illustrations for the Island of Balance that we can offer, is the fact that there are two of us communicating with you right now. One of us possesses more "male" energy, (Pete) while the other possesses more "female" energy (Mejik). Just like the differences in our personalities, these differences in energies are meant to *complement*. They are not meant to be automatically defined in terms of value; one being better than another. In your society, we can see where these mistaken value judgements play a part. They exist each time people choose to believe that one gender is better overall, than the other gender. But those who are in touch with their own Island of Balance understand that no one thing is better than another. They understand that it is the *differences* between them that can constructively come together to create Balance.

Suppose there are two people involved in a situation of domestic violence. The individual who inflicts the harm on the other does so because she/he is not in touch with her/his Island of Balance enough to understand the role of the other individual. The violent attitude that one individual takes toward another is an example of what can happen when we choose not to recognize the complementary elements that exist within others, and prefer instead to concentrate on things that we feel we alone have a right to, or we alone can do better than anyone else. By robbing ourselves of the opportunity to receive complementary aspects from others, we become very unhappy. In some cases this unhappiness causes us to become violent. Children often display this character when they sense their feelings being threatened. If a child feels that he needs something but is not getting it, he forgets to recognize the need for complementary Balance and shuts down his own flow of energy so as not to connect with others. Often this takes the form of tantrums and eventually violence toward others if connections are not reestablished. Although this can sometimes be seen in children more easily, it exists in anyone who disconnects themselves from their Island of Balance.

By shutting down the pathways that connect us to others, we fail to understand what it is we need to truly be happy. Being in touch with our

Island of Balance allows us to examine all aspects of ourselves so that we can see where we might benefit from understanding or sensing things through the Islands of others.

If you feel through the area of your heart, as explained in previous Islands, you would benefit from meeting someone whose connections to the world were centered around their heads. This does not mean that you must change the way that you think or feel, or the way that you interpret information in the world around you. It simply means that since your "scales" are tipped in the direction of the heart, a person whose scales are tipped toward their mind would help you to see things in a different way. This understanding would not only allow you to grasp the reasoning behind others' perceptions, but would also put you in the position of developing a Balance within yourself. If we all developed this sense of Balance within ourselves, and learned to reach out to the Islands of others for enlightenment, domestic violence cases (actually *all* cases of violence) would cease to exist. Each of us would feel the need to do whatever was necessary to *understand* the other, instead of forcing the other to experience our own unhappiness that resulted when we disconnected from our Island of Balance.

Think about what happens within you when you hear someone speak about another and use such words as "mentally imbalanced" to describe them. Often we think that those among us who are considered unbalanced mentally, are suffering because they have not mastered the art of living in a way that conforms to this society. And because we tend to identify so strongly with our mental faculties, we assume the imbalance exists in this area. But in order to fully understand the nature of the imbalance, we must consider that in order for there to be an upset or imbalance in this area, it must be judged against energy from another area.

The energy that exists in the area of the head/mind, cannot be considered unbalanced in itself because it cannot be weighed against itself. This does not imply that there cannot exist a physical condition that does not allow for proper brain function, ("proper" here refers to the rules of the society in which you live) but what we are discussing is directly related to energy.

Because society's teaching tells us the brain has two halves, we assume that an imbalance can exist between them. However, when we are discussing the relation of energy, we refer to the area of the brain as one form of energy. Therefore, in order to create an imbalance with this energy, we would need to measure it against energy from other areas such as the heart or hands (feeling). Let us examine this.

Imagine for a moment that you have been told a friend of yours is "mentally imbalanced". You have known this friend for a long time, and have noticed recently that something has been "wrong" with her. You have observed changes in her behavior, and you have also sensed that she is not as happy as she had been in the past. Perhaps you have tried talking to your friend in an effort to get her to tell you what has been bothering her, but she does not admit that she is bothered by anything. The fact is, she senses you may be attempting to put yourself in a position that would force her to divulge what she is feeling or thinking, and another part of her (another area of energy) does not want this to surface. Instead of trying to reach a Balance between all of her energies, she denies she has lost touch with a certain one, and shies away from you in order to keep her secret. The more people who choose to confront your friend, the more she retreats until she becomes so overwhelmed with trying to deny the part of herself that needs to be put back *in* Balance, that she falls further and further *out* of Balance.

Let us set up a scenario in which this explanation could have happened.

Suppose your friend had always lived in a way that put emotional feelings high on her list of priorities in decision making. At some point in her life, she took a job that required she make decisions solely from an intellectual standpoint. She is not to consider the emotional feelings of her co-workers when she makes her decisions, even though these decisions directly effect those around her. She knows that if she stays with this job, she will be going against her personal Truth. But often we tend to make excuses for why we stay with things that rob us of our true happiness, and this is the case with your friend. For her own reasons, she has managed to justify why she should stay with her present situation. Perhaps she convinces herself that it is only temporary until something "better" comes along. But as we all should understand at this point in our trip through our Islands, nothing just "comes along". We have to make a choice to acquire what we need, and we do this by reconnecting to the energy within and around us.

With each work day that passes, your friend loses touch with what she needs to remain happy. She can no longer use the energy around her heart to make decisions at work, and must rely on the energy around her head. Before she came to work where she does, she had been able to utilize both centers of energy effectively. Even though she prioritized one form over the other, she maintained a Balance by not allowing one to completely overpower the other. Now, in her present situation, she has no choice but to allow one to dominate the other. Even worse for her, is the one that must do the dominating is not the one she would have chosen for herself.

As your friend spends more and more time going against her personal sense of Truth, and thus losing touch with that Island that keeps her in Balance, parts of her entire being begin to change. While her boss might see these changes as good, in the sense that she can now rely on your friend to function in the way that was mentioned earlier, you, as well as other close acquaintances, see these changes for what they truly are; very bad for your friend and those around her. Since you have known your friend for longer than her boss has, you understand what had made her happy in the past, and can see the unhappiness that now manifests. The boss sees only that what she wants is being carried out in the manner prescribed, and does not know your friend well enough to comprehend the possibility of unhappiness. After all, if your friend stays with the job and performs the way she should, what reason would the boss have to question things? But you, and many others know your friend is unhappy. At some level your friend also knows this, but hides it behind excuses. This could go on indefinitely, and often does until Balance is thrown off, and things change so drastically that your friend has no choice but to confront the imbalance within her.

This need for confrontation is not always realized however, until the person tips her own energy scales so far over that others must be brought in to assist them in reestablishing their sense of Balance. In more serious cases, this is referred to as a "nervous breakdown", but sometimes it is seen only as a "mental imbalance" since others tend to remain focused on the physical condition of the brain as described earlier. There *is* an imbalance, but it is not of the purely physical/mental kind.

If your friend realizes on her own that she is not happy, and is determined to make the changes necessary to renew her happiness, then she will not slip so far off Balance that she needs help getting back. If however, she allows the personal Truth of another (in our example, we would say the boss's sense of Truth, which would focus on the energy around the head) to encapsulate her own Truth, (emotional feeling) she may not know how to release herself from this grasp. When the scales tip so far in this direction that a person does not even realize they are not working within the realms of their own sense of Truth, the energy from the Island of Balance attempts to correct the situation. Should this happen, your friend might experience episodes of euphoria, coupled with devastation. Or they might act "inappropriately" in any given situation, such as laughing uncontrollably when they are supposed to be serious. Such behavior tempts others to say that they are not Balanced.

Each of the previously mentioned examples offers proof of what can happen when we are forced to compromise our sense of Truth, and we allow one part of our selves to take over. The parts of our selves we had attempted to deny, push their way through in ways that are not always "appropriate", because the need to maintain a Balance is too strong. The places in which we had denied our energies access to Balance, come through the strongest. That is why your friend might laugh at a serious meeting, or during times that are traditionally sad. Her sense of Balance is telling her she needs to see the humor in all situations, and if she cannot see it in a way that would be considered "Balanced" then it will come through in ways that are not always so.

Experiencing two very different emotions at the same time, is also a call from the Island of Balance to reconnect with it. If your friend did indeed experience a state of euphoria within moments of experiencing devastation, she should know this is one of the most simplistic calls for Balance. When we experience what we would perceive as two very different, or opposite feelings, thoughts, etc., we are being called to place them in their appropriate positions, allowing one to complement the other. Once we acknowledge this calling, we must take the measures necessary to reconnect to the Island that helps us recapture this state.

How to Gain Access to the Island of Balance

As we visited the previous Islands, you might have noticed that visual imagery and meditation have been of great importance in reconnecting to them. In order to reconnect with the Island of Balance however, a slightly different approach must be applied.

Because the Island of Balance is one that connects all other Islands through its ability to incorporate one with another, you must re-learn how to connect with those parts of your selves that you employ in this existence. Therefore, we will not focus primarily on the mental realm of imagery and meditation to reconnect with the energies within and around us. In our quest to reconnect with this Island and the next, we will also be reaching out to the physical world to gain an understanding of what we receive from it.

Balance between all things happens as a result of energies being exchanged or transferred. Each time we see another human, an animal, or even a plant in distress, the sadness we feel within us is actually energy, and part of that energy is automatically transferred to the being in distress. The same is true when we witness another's happiness. If we feel happy for them, they can sense this. And if we feel jealous as a result of their happiness, they will be aware of this as well. Even if they do not respond to these feelings on a conscious level, they will know they exist because as energies are transferred, they will feel more or less happiness in our presence. When we examine what occurs between the energies within us, we come to realize the same type of exchange or transfer is taking place around us. For example, we may feel within our heart energy that we really should be happy for a friend of ours who just bought a new house. But the energy that is our brain/mind, begins to offer us reasons not to be happy for this friend. Even though your particular sense of Truth may lie within the area of your heart, the contradictory energy of your head creates an atmosphere of imbalance. We can see that different types of energy are being transferred, but these particular types are not the most beneficial ones for us. What we need is to create an atmosphere in which the energies within us come into Balance in a way that creates happiness within our being. Once we have accomplished this, and have reconnected to the Island of Balance within ourselves, we can proceed to reconnect through a state of Balance to the world around us.

For the next few days, keep track of the feelings that you experience. Do not simply acknowledge them, but be sure to write them down as well. One of the steps to reconnecting to your Island of Balance, is being able to remember when and why you experienced the feelings that you did. You cannot hope to remember all of them, (at a conscious level) as well as the circumstances that brought them about, if you do not keep a record of them.

In your record book, document as much as you can to explain what was happening around the time you noticed you were feeling a particular way. Besides your feelings of happiness, sadness, worry, jealousy, guilt, etc., record the events that had happened prior to this. Did you see or talk with anyone? Were you just told you had to do something that you really did not want to do? Did you do something you now feel guilty about? Notice when you ask yourself these questions, and others like them, if you are able to answer them right away or if one part of you tries to answer and another part tries to suppress the answer. Use the meditation techniques discussed in previous sections to visit both the parts of yourself that want to answer, and those that do not. Try to find out why there is a conflict. You may not have the time to do the meditation at the moment you become aware of this conflict, so recording it and attempting to find the answer later will be of great benefit.

Do not feel that you are limited in your recording however. Everything that took place up to the point you noticed a particular feeling welling-up inside of you, is important. The more details you can record, the easier it will be for you later. After you have written the most obvious events, concentrate on the ones that may have been less obvious. For instance, you might want to ask yourself what the weather was like, or how hot/cold it was. Were you enclosed in a tiny space with no windows, or were you outside in the fresh air with a beautiful view in front of you? All of these things, as well as elements in your personal experiences, are items to consider when recording your feelings. Because all things contain energy at different levels, the amount that can be transferred varies. And not all forms of energy are the type we would like to accept. If, for example, it was thundering and lightening at a time when you felt very happy, this would indicate that the energy charge within the storm actually played a part in boosting your own energy levels. Because you were in a state of Balance within your self, (evidenced by happiness) you were better able to project this state of Balance to the world around you; in this case, the atmosphere. You were able to accept the energy that surrounded you and that would add to your happiness You were also able to transfer those energies that you no longer needed (in other words, those that might have made you unhappy). In doing so, you would have allowed different sources to draw from those energies what *they* needed, just as you had taken what you required. On the other hand, if you noticed you felt frightened or anxious during this storm, it was because of an imbalance that existed within you. The energy that was created as a result of different parts of yourself clashing, was multiplied as a result of the storm. Without being consciously aware of it, the energies within you called out to another energy source the way two warring parties would call out to a third, seemingly neutral party for a satisfactory resolution. But instead of this outside energy being able to help your situation when it transferred energy to you, it was only able to add to the feeling(s) that already existed. Thus, you became frightened or anxious as a result. Unless you are willing to take personal responsibility for a resolution, all of the energy that exists around you will do nothing for you but add to your present dilemma.

Throughout your recordings, it will also help you to jot down the colors you are wearing, as well as those colors that you might have encountered repeatedly before your feeling developed. Color plays a very important role in our moods/feelings because of the energy that it lends. Many doctors and therapists in your society have come to understand the roles colors play, but these judgments are in no way meant to be absolute answers for each and every one of us. Some individuals feel comfort around the color blue, while others detest it. There are many reasons as to why people feel differently about the same color. The best and most reliable source for this answer, as well as the answers to all of the questions you must ask yourself, is *you*.

Once you have compiled your list of feelings/moods, and the events, scenes, weather, colors, and any other pertinent information associated with them, put some time aside and review it. Try to find the patterns that exist before moving on to meditation. Often just being able to review what you have written, is enough to help you gain a better understanding of where you need to put things into Balance. Notice recurring colors, weather patterns, people you have encountered in association with partic-ular moods. Then examine from where the feelings associated with these items appear to emanate. If you notice that bringing any of these things into focus again creates a "warring" effect between two or more parts of you, then concentrate on those parts. Learn how to differentiate between the part of you that feels Truth, and that part which would prefer to block your personal Truth from surfacing by causing unhappy thoughts/feelings. If you are having a difficult time telling the difference, it might mean that you need to delve into these parts through meditation. Look back to the section on Quality and follow those steps. In addition, the following guidelines will be helpful to you.

If you have opted to try to find your answers through meditation, and have reread the section on Quality, you will have no trouble at all recon-necting with your Island of Balance. Begin by sensing the energy within each part of your being. Then, concentrate on the parts that appear to be causing your conflict. When you have reached the area that is the source of your Truth, you will know it because visiting this area will cause you to experience great happiness. Stay with this feeling of happiness until you feel confident you know all you can about it. Without allowing the source of conflict to intrude, feel what it would be like to make decisions or to replay what has caused you unhappiness in the past, with the aid of this energy alone. Let yourself feel the happiness associated with this, while you deny access to the source of conflict.

Once you understand the source of your sense of True happiness, move your concentration to the center of the conflict. Ask yourself why you allow these feelings of unhappiness to intrude upon your sense of happiness. Perhaps the answer exists in the recent past, or perhaps it exists in a past life. With a little time, the answer will become apparent.

Now that you understand what you need to experience happiness, as well as why you allow other parts of yourself to sabotage this happiness, you can begin to create a needed Balance. Begin your quest for Balance by continuing your meditation. Imagine your sense of Truth and your source of conflict meeting. See each of them as round or egg-shaped spheres of light. Do not be concerned if one light is brighter than the other. Often this happens when we are out of Balance. Imagine each of the spheres meeting one another at a point that is somewhere between the two. Hold their energy there for a while, allowing them to weave with each other. You can assist by imagining yourself weaving them together, or performing a similar task that would result in them mixing energies.

After you have successfully woven, mixed, or meshed these energies together, and you feel confident they are part of one another, move the energy from the place it had occupied to the area that is your personal source of Truth. When the energy reaches this position, see and feel it surge with happiness. It can do this because it has reached the point within you where it needs to be in order to be happy and not cause future conflicts. Next, replay the event that caused you the conflict in the first place, but imagine it from the point of view of your freshly Balanced source of Truth. Do not allow the energy that had caused the conflict to escape and return to its previous dwelling. Remember that it once occupied the place where it now rests, so in a sense it has come "home", thanks to you.

By pulling the source of conflict back to its location with your personal sense of Truth, you have created an opening for the correct energy to fill. The place that had once been your source of conflict, can now be replenished with energy that is meant to work in accordance with the center of Truth, thereby creating Balance. You should no longer feel forced to experience unhappiness as a result of a particular area vying for power. Instead, you will experience what it is like to work within the Island of Balance, and remain open only to *suggestion* from other areas. And once you have learned to understand and work with Balance, you can easily apply it to the world around you.

Reconnecting with the Island of Balance, or any Island for that matter, does not simply imply that you work with the energies within your self, and ignore those energies around you. Although the previous Islands have focused on the work you needed to do within yourself, part of working with the Island of Balance should have made you aware of the work you must do in the world around you in order to feel happiness within. With the lesson of this Island fresh within ourselves, we move onto the next Island; the Island of Perception.

THE ISLAND
OF
PERCEPTION

Thou shalt be happy!
Mejik

What is the first thing you think of when we mention the word "Perception"? Do you automatically think of the way you view the world around you? If this was your first thought, you are correct. However, if this was not your first thought, you are also correct. You cannot be wrong for the way you perceive the reality that you have created. This is exactly what the Island of Perception is all about.

Throughout the previous chapters, you have learned that the main objective of the energy that is you, is to be happy. This is your Will, your inner Truth, and must be recognized and honored in order for you to live a life of Quality, Love, Balance, etc. But exactly what items in your life do you Perceive as sources of happiness? If you take the time to contemplate these items, you will undoubtedly discover that you adopted at least some of them from friends, family, or even society in general. Before any of us can delve deeper into our Island of Perception, we must learn to separate those things that make us happy in accordance with our inner Truth, from those which have brought us happiness only because we convinced ourselves they should.

Let us assume that you live in a society where children are desired. Let us also assume that the population where you live would not suffer if people chose to produce less children. In fact, the Earth would probably benefit from having less humans to sustain. You and your partner have been discussing the possibility of having children. Neither one of you has firmly decided whether you would like to have them or not. But it is important to realize that if both of you are not in touch with your own inner Truth, you will be lead to a decision based upon the feelings of others. This cannot benefit anyone involved since it goes against what *you* need to create happiness. Let us look at this through an example.

You are in the process of deciding whether you want children, or not. Perhaps certain family members expect you to produce children. Each of them has their own reasons for feeling this way. Some of them merely have not thought much about an alternative, and Perceive their happiness in this world inclusive of children. Others might think that a family name needs to be preserved, thus ensuring their, or some other member of the family's happiness. Still others have their own reasons, which they are entitled to have provided they do not attempt to push these ideas onto you or anyone else. You see, each of these people has formulated their own opinions based upon those things they feel will bring them happiness. Whether these things actually do bring them the happiness they strive for, depends on whether they are in touch with their own Islands of Perception. One positive way to determine if they are in touch with this Island, is to examine the way they handle your situation.

A person who is in touch with their Island of Perception will understand that you are entitled to make your own decisions based upon your own inner Truth. They will be comfortable enough with the decisions they have made in their own lives, which have brought them the happiness they Perceived. As we mentioned earlier, they will understand that even if the choices that you make are different from their own, you are not wrong. On the other hand, someone who is *not* in touch with their Island of Perception is equally easy to distinguish. These people feel it is necessary to force their opinions on others. Many times they do not recognize they have a choice, and therefore cannot fathom that you have a choice in matters as well. They base their happiness on their ability to perform those things in life that they are expected to do in accordance with society's rules, family rules, etc. Many of them cannot admit they are not truly happy. They feel that to admit something like this would be similar to telling the world they failed to be true to themselves, so they continue to convince themselves that any decisions they make actually do provide them with some form of happiness.

It is important to understand that if someone truly does feel happiness, even if they appear to be following what is expected of them, they have tapped into their sense of Truth, and are much better for it than someone who must convince themselves they are happy. This is because convincing the energy of the mind that we are happy, does not convince the rest of the energy within and around us. Although this person may manage to create a facade of happiness for their mind to look through, it is almost impossible for them to create such opposition to their inner Truth from all places, including their Islands.

When we choose to work against the Truth within our Islands, the energy within and around us knows this. If we analyze the previous example, we can easily see three generally separate forces at work. First, there is you, the undecided individual. We would say that you are the neutral party. Furthermore, there exist two types of energy, largely in opposition to one another. One group of energy wants to force you into making a decision based upon what it feels is best, and the other group wants to allow you to create your own happiness based upon your inner sense of Truth. If you are not in touch with your Islands, mainly your Island of Perception, you create openings for the opinions of others to seep through. And without the power that comes from a secure sense of your Island of Perception, those opinions can produce enough energy to make you feel you need to follow them in order to attain happiness.

Just as the energy that is in and around us knows when we choose to work against our own sense of Truth, it is also keenly aware of others around us who are operating in this way. Think of people who you have encountered who have made you feel uneasy or annoyed because each time you tried to talk with them, they tried to convince you that the way *they* Perceived the world was the way that *you* should Perceive it. If you were even the slightest bit in tune with your Island of Perception, you would have felt the energy within or around some part of your body being agitated when this person spoke. This is because your energy recognized that the forceful energy exuding from this person was the result of their being out-of-touch with the source of their own True happiness. In their presence, your own energies would have set up a defense barrier that allowed you to listen to their opinions and to maintain an "open mind", but would have kept them from influencing you in any way.

Although each decision we make must be made in accordance with our own Island of Perception in order for us to be truly happy, this does not mean that each of us cannot benefit from the opinions of others. As we become more intimately involved with our Island of Perception, we begin to seek out the company of friends, relatives, or acquaintances who seem to know intuitively what it is we need to be happy. These are not those individuals who we mentioned before; those who would prefer to force their opinions on you. Instead, these individuals are genuinely concerned with your feelings, and sense what you need to be happy. These people are not only in touch with their own Islands of Perception, but understand how to connect their energy to yours, thus pulling to the surface the answers to the happiness you sought all along.

Individuals who display the type of behavior that comes as a result of being in touch with their own Islands, as well as the Islands of others, will not demand that their words be followed. They will choose instead, to offer suggestions when asked. Let us assist you in understanding what we mean.

Pretend that you are confused about your job. Your present position has brought anxiety, sadness, even anger into your life, and you are suffering as a result. The individual with whom you share your work, thrives under this type of pressure and anxiety, so you stick with your job, convincing your mind that the problem must lie within yourself since after all, this other person can perform her/his job perfectly well. But as we had mentioned before, the reason this person performs well under the same pressure that causes you to fizzle, is because they have a different sense of Perception. Their own Islands tell them that this is how a job should be, and they derive happiness from this type of work because they are working in accordance with what they believe. You on the other hand, do not Perceive things the same way, and the same type of work does not cause you the same happiness that your co-worker feels. You begin to think about changing jobs, but are held back for several reasons. You may think your present job pays very well, or you might find the hours convenient. Perhaps you have recognized the possibility that you do not move to a new position because of the inadequacies you Perceive you possess. You contemplate your choices, and finally enlist the aid of a close friend.

This friend has always been a willing listener. He does not tell you what you should do, but offers suggestions that he feels might be beneficial for you. As you speak to him concerning the way you feel about your job, he senses that you are not following your inner Truth. He picks up on the energy you are exuding, and realizes you do not want to stay in your present position. But instead of admitting this consciously, you have set up barriers of excuses that are keeping you from allowing yourself to follow your own path to happiness. Without telling you what you *should* do, your friend offers his opinion, which is based upon what he feels you truly desire to do, but have been denying. In other words, he is giving you the same answer that you would have arrived at on your own, had you been better in touch with your own Islands, specifically the Island of Perception. You will know that the thoughts which your friend voiced are really your own, when you begin to consider them. If you picture yourself acting out the scenario set fourth by your friend, (assuming your friend not only suggested you change jobs, but also helped you by assisting you in acknowledging other types of jobs that would be better suited for you) you will feel a growing sense of happiness. This is how you know you are regaining a connection to your Island of Perception, and ultimately, your sense of Truth.

How to Gain Access to the Island of Perception

One of the best ways to determine if you have learned the lessons associated with the previous Islands, is to take notice of how easy it is for you to access your Island of Perception. If you have truly grasped the lessons you were meant to learn, in other words if you are now reaping the benefits from the connections you made to your other Islands, then reconnecting to your Island of Perception will be almost elementary. If on the other hand, you have skipped through this book and chosen not to completely connect to all of your Islands, then creating a connection to this one will be difficult.

To fully access your Island of Perception, it might help to look over the items you recorded as part of the exercise discussed in the previous chapter. Identify those items which allowed you to experience happiness, and concentrate on the feeling(s) they elicit. Imagine yourself performing, creating, observing, or doing whatever it is that causes you to feel happy. Imagine all parts of the scene as you had written them down. Know that you are also free to add more if you choose. Hold this image until you are confident you have truly acknowledged and accepted the happiness you are experiencing as a result of it. Without releasing the image, begin to Perceive other parts of your life as they fit into this scene. For example, you may have conjured an image of yourself hiking in the mountains because this act brings you happiness. However, you are in the same unhappy situation as our earlier example illustrated when it comes to your present profession. Instead of allowing the negativity and unhappiness of the latter situation to effect the happiness within your imaginings, hold fast to the scene depicting the mountains, and mingle this setting, a little at a time, with the image you hold of your job. This is the same principle you would use if you were to bake a cake or mix chemicals. Certain ingredients need to be combined slowly in order for them not to cause unwanted results. Let us go further in the example we just mentioned to help you understand fully what we mean.

Let us say that you have a wonderful mountainous scene in the realms of your imagination at this very moment. You stand in full hiking gear, on the side of a mountain somewhere in this world or any other. (Remember, however you wish to imagine it is entirely up to you. Your inner sense of Truth might lead you to places you have not experienced physically, and that is perfectly all right.) Around you are plush, green trees, and somewhere in the distance you hear the rush of water from a mountain stream. You notice the sounds of birds approaching, and look to the sun-filled sky as they fly above you to places unknown. Ahead of you there is a clearing, and from this point you are able to see for miles and miles. Small animals cross your path now and then, none of them threatening in any way. You are happy, and you feel at peace.

Without letting go of this image, you begin to add people, events, and feelings associated with your present job. Perhaps you remember an event that happened just a few days ago when you were forced, against your Will, so-to-speak, to stay at work late and miss a very meaningful award ceremony in which someone very close to you was being honored. Think of how this made you feel, but do not allow the feeling to overwhelm the happiness you are experiencing within the mountains. Remain within the scene you have created, and place this one event somewhere within that scene. (Do not attempt to work on more than one event at a time, or you will not receive the benefits of this exercise.)

The work related event that you have placed within your scene of the mountains, can manifest in a variety of ways. You may notice it immediately if you step back and look at yourself as part of your imaginings to see that a sad, or down-cast look has replaced the peaceful, happy look that once was visible on your face. You may even notice the event manifesting somewhere in the environment that surrounds you. Sometimes this can take the shape of a threatening animal, an earthquake, or even turbulent waters. As always, there are infinite possibilities. If something does not seem "right" about your scene, it is up to you to delve deeper into its meaning through your work with the Islands. No matter how you Perceive this event however, know that it can be changed to fit into the more desirous scene that you created.

If we say the event gave you an unhappy expression for example, force yourself to look around you at the things that made you feel happy when you first imagined them. Since you alone were in charge of their placement, you knew how to draw the correct energies as well as the things associated with them, into your scene. Knowing this, you must also acknowledge that you have the power to allow these happier energies to dissolve the less-than-happy event. If you look around you at the wonderful things that exist for you, you will feel the sadness, guilt, or whatever emotion you did not desire to feel, turning itself into a more desirable one.

If you did not see a change in yourself in the scene we just mentioned, but instead imagined the event as a decaying tree or threatening animal, you can also find the path to change this. The way the tree looks, and the threat of the animal represent the way that you feel. These feelings are the result of the action you chose to take which ultimately went against your Will; your inner sense of Truth and happiness. But now that you have brought this event into your scene, you have the power to change it by changing the way that it manifested.

Suppose you saw the tree in the way we just described. You might choose to carefully examine the tree in an attempt to discover what is wrong with it. By asking yourself questions such as, "What happened to make the tree look like this?", or, "Is there anything this tree needs to feel and look better?" you are actually trying to determine what *you* need to feel better about the event with which you are working. The same type of questions would apply if you were faced with a threatening animal. The fear you feel in the presence of this animal is actually the fear of what will happen to you if you continue to stray from your inner sense of Truth. Do not be afraid to confront the animal to determine what you need. If you approach it calmly, it will respond calmly. Since what exists in your scene is created by you, it must make sense to you that the way you desire to approach this animal will also be the way that the animal responds to you. Once contact has been made and you have received the answers you were looking for, bring together the animal, tree, or whatever it may be, in a way that adds to your happiness. See yourself walking with the animal, petting the animal, or watching it go back into the woods in a calm manner. Imagine yourself watering the tree to bring it back to its original self, or removing any vines that might be inhibiting its growth. Then see the tree fitting into your scene in a way that brings you happiness. You will know you have accomplished this when you see that wonderful look of happiness on your face, and you feel the same sense of tranquillity that you felt when you first imagined the scene.

It is important for you not to give up if the answers do not come immediately. As with any Island, it takes some time to reconnect. And if you are used to veering from your path of true happiness, it may take some time to realize what you need to truly be happy. The key to reconnecting however, is to make sure you do not bombard yourself with too many unhappy events at one time. Create your scene of happiness, and then slowly add one item at a time until you feel comfortable enough with that item to move onto the next. Once you have mastered this lesson, you can consider yourself back in touch with your Island of Perception, and therefore ready to move onto the final Island; the Island of Nothingness.

THE ISLAND
OF
NOTHINGNESS

If we work backwards from where we began, it is the source of reality.
Pete

Here, within the Island of Nothingness, we come full-circle. Through our visits to our Islands, we have become aware of the magnanimous energy that exists within each of us, as well as the pathways necessary to reconnect to this power. We have learned what constitutes our personal sense of Truth, and have taken on the responsibility of manifesting that Truth by acknowledging that each of us has the right to her/his own reality. But this final Island does not imply an ending. Rather, it is as the statement above declares, a source. In other words, we cannot simply look at these seven Islands as a straight line that must be kept in order. Although it is important to learn the lessons of each Island as we have presented them in this book, it is less important to always follow them in this specific order. If you picture these Islands as a circular configuration, you will better understand what we mean. Provided you have learned the lessons associated with each of the Islands as they were presented to you, you will understand that should you need to refresh your connections in the future, (and we almost always need refreshing at some point) you may begin with any Island that you consider appropriate.

Suppose that you feel you are not connecting with your Island of Beauty. You have been noticing items of ugliness or beauty in your life, and find that you are having a hard time accessing the reasons why you feel as you do toward these items. You do not need to read through the previous Islands in order to reconnect to this Island, since you have already recognized the Island with which you need to work. But included in the lessons you have learned, is the belief that each of these Islands is not separate. Each one connects to the others, therefore creating an overall connection within each individual. So if you begin your future work within the Island of Beauty, you are doing so with the awareness that you still maintain a connection to the other Islands. Let us use an illustration to better exemplify this.

If we imagine our Islands as seven figures that create a circle, we can easily see that no Island offers us a definite beginning, and no Island offers us a definite ending. We choose the Islands we wish to visit, in the order we wish to visit them, once we have established our initial connection. Should we choose in our future connections to begin with the Island of Beauty, we must also be aware that this Island is part of a greater whole. To choose a point on the circle not only makes us aware that an endless connection of Islands exist, but it also prompts us to recognize the path that an understanding of our connections has created. It begins to become clear to us that if we commence work at a certain point on this circle, we will eventually come back to that point; hence the saying in your society, "Coming full-circle."

Undoubtedly some who read this book will question what will happen if you choose to work within one Island and not follow the pathway of the circle. We must impress upon you the fact that it is not entirely possible to work within the confines of one Island. Each Island is created with the energies of the Islands that surround it, so no Island is complete by itself. If you have been following this book closely you may have already realized this, as each section leads you toward the next Island. Without the understanding of the Island before it and after it, the Island you wish to explore will never be fully mastered. To put it quite simply, an Island alone is Nothing.

Think of yourself as compared to your friends. Do not seek to compare yourself in ways that make you feel less adequate, but compare yourself in ways that are simply different. Ask yourself questions about your physical attributes, or even about your chosen profession. Do you have brown hair? Does your friend have brown hair also? If so, would you consider yours more "mousy", or more "chocolate-colored"? Have you chosen a profession that allows you to work outdoors, yet have a friend who has chosen an office job, and another one who has chosen to stay at home and raise a family? The reason you can make the distinction between these things is because you are not working alone. The very definition of "compare" suggests a relationship between two or more things. Since we cannot successfully compare something to itself, we invent definitions to describe the differences, and even similarities that we discover when we work with two or more items.

The energy that makes a branch a branch and a leaf a leaf, is different because we see them as having different physical traits, but all are part of one whole (the tree). If we could communicate with the branch or the leaf, and we asked them how they compared themselves to each other, we would find that unlike each of us, they could not answer this. They do not understand that they are separate parts of one whole. They only understand that they exist. This is the same concept put forth in our illustration of our Islands. Although each Island has a main core, and therefore a different title, each is undeniably part of a whole. These Islands within us do not acknowledge that they exist independent of the others. Like the tree and the leaf, they simply recognize that they exist, each lending energy from its core, and borrowing energy from the cores of others in order to complete the circle, and therefore the whole.

When the Islands within us go unrecognized, that is to say when we break our connections with them, they continue to perform this transference of energy. However, since this activity is beyond our comprehension at the time, we do not completely benefit from it. When we do finally reconnect to our Islands, it is as though we are being presented with seven plain canvasses. We are then asked what we desire to create on each canvas. To put this another way, we are asked to manifest our sense of Truth as it becomes apparent. We are asked to create our own reality. And finally, we are called upon to recognize that which is our very essence; the ability to create from, and exist within Nothingness.

Since this is an excellent time to offer an example, we choose to do so.

Suppose that you are part of a group that is offered a blank book and a writing instrument. Your assignment is to fill the book with any form of writing that you wish, as long as what is contained within its pages can fit within the confines of one title. Some of those who received this assignment will create a book of poems, others will create short stories, a few will create novels that fill the book, and perhaps other volumes as well. Some may even choose to copy sayings or poems from other sources. Although the final product will be different for all involved, you must consider that each of you was given the same tools to begin your work. This is how the Island of Nothingness operates. To learn the lessons of this Island you must be willing to accept the fact that you alone are in charge of your sense of Truth, and therefore your sense of reality.

As we told you in the very beginning of this book, each of us holds seven Island within ourselves. When we begin to feel their gentle stirrings, and we recognize that they exist, we take the steps that are necessary to access them. At this point, they are our blank books. What we choose to write becomes our recognition of our sense of Truth, and we weed out those things that we previously had chosen to borrow from others. We understand our essence, our true path, when we sense the power within each of our Islands and we form our sense of reality. Even though we are all operating with the same tools, (Islands) what we choose to create when we put them together, turns out to be very different.

If you consider the feelings you had at the beginning of each of the sections of this book, you will be better able to identify with our example of the blank book. As you were being reintroduced to your Islands, you were being given the gift of Nothingness. You were being asked to accept the

Islands within yourself, and to create something on each canvas as it presented itself. Now, having done just that, you are being given this gift all over again. You can choose to link the Island of Nothingness to your other Islands, thus completing the circle, and feel the surge of power that comes with the understanding of what it is like to exist in a state of true happiness, defined by Nothing but your own sense of reality.

How to Gain Access to the Island of Nothingness

In order to access and reap the benefits inherent in your Island of Nothingness, you must have learned how to reconnect with all of the Islands we mentioned in previous sections. If you know that you have skipped through this book without reconnecting as fully as you should, it would be beneficial for you to go back through each section and perform the exercises listed under "Getting Back In Touch…" If, on the other hand you feel that you are ready to move onto this final Island and link all of the other Islands together, you may do so through the following exercises. We must tell you however, that these final exercises will be slightly different than those which you have encountered in previous sections. These exercises are not geared toward a reconnection to a part of your self, but toward a total connection to all that exists within you and the world outside your physical body.

The first step in getting back in touch with your Island of Nothingness, requires that you take a few moments to close your eyes and imagine the circular configuration of Islands that we mentioned earlier in this section. Remember that because these Islands are your own, you can picture them in any shape, color, or form that your imagination allows. What is important in that you are able to imagine them.

Do not attempt to place the seventh Island, the Island of Nothingness into this pattern until the image you hold of the other six Islands is absolutely clear. When your image is finally strong, place the Island of Nothingness in its appropriate location. Some individuals might see the Island as a puzzle piece that interlocks with the others. Other individuals will see this final Island as a shape that emerges to fill in a blank spot in their circle. Some may even see this as a larger Island that surfaces within the center of the circle to tie all of the others together. Remember that any way you picture this image is perfectly correct.

Once this Island is positioned in a place that seems correct to you, see the energy that is this Island moving toward the other Islands. Imagine each Island in turn, moving their energy to the next. If you are attempting to envision this energy, but are having difficulty doing so, it may help to assign colors to your Islands. As you move energies from one Island to the other, it sometimes helps to see these energies as shifting colors. Let us use an example to illustrate this.

To keep this example short, we will pretend that there are only three Islands. Let us use the Islands of Quality, Love, and Knowledge. Suppose that you see the Island of Quality as red, the Island of Love as Pink, and the Island of Knowledge as Purple. Now imagine them in a circular pattern. When this image is clear within your mind, your heart, or within the area you choose as its origination, picture part of the color red from the first Island reaching out to the next in the form of a hand, a key, or even a big blob. Once the red energy has reached the pink energy, (Love) imagine the two colors mixing together. Be careful not to allow one color to blend completely with another. It is important to always be able to decipher one color, and therefore one energy, from another. This is to ensure that one Island does not gain precedence over another, and that they work in harmony with each other.

Once you have managed to create the image of red mixing successfully with pink, picture a bit of pink energy from the Island of Love mixing with the purple energy of your Island of Knowledge. Finally, take the purple energy of Knowledge and mix it with the red energy of Quality. Go through this same procedure over and over again until each Island contains all of the colors that you had originally chosen. It helps to take a look at all of your Islands when you reach the final one in order to discover which colors are missing. In our example, purple has not been applied to the Island of Love, so that is one of the energies that we need to move *directly from the Island of its origin.* It is important not to create a criss-cross pattern between Islands. This creates too much frenzied energy. Instead, move the purple energy through the Island of Quality, to the Island of Love by following the same circular line that you created initially. You will know that you have successfully completed this process when you are able to imagine all of your Islands containing all of the colors you had originally chosen. When you have successfully envisioned your Islands in this way, you have completed the first step toward connecting with your Island of Nothingness. By allowing yourself to mix the colors of your Islands, you have acknowledged that no one Island can exist without the efforts and the energies of the others. Without the others, any one Island is Nothing.

The next step in reconnecting with your Island of Nothingness, requires reconnections to the Islands of others. Just as we learned how to mix our own energies, we will learn how we can combine our energies with the energies of others in order to produce a desired reality. As we had mentioned earlier in this section, we have come full-circle, and are now ready to acknowledge that without a connection to all energy, including the energy of others, we are Nothing. We cannot completely understand ourselves unless we learn to understand others as well.

At this point in your journey, you must acknowledge that your Islands, although different from the Islands of other individuals, are capable of mixing with them. Whenever you feel the need for better communication between you and another individual, simply picture your Islands blending with theirs. Do not worry that you will not be able to do this if they have not been in touch with their own Islands, or that they must tell you their own personal colors in order for you to create your mixture. With the understanding that you have attained, you are perfectly capable of creating a connection without their help. Let us explain what we mean.

Suppose you have not been completely honest with a friend of yours, and you have been feeling bad about this. Your friend probably realizes at some level that something is wrong, but when they approach you to ask you what is wrong, you pretend that there is no problem. This dishonesty is creating discord between you and your friend, but at the present moment you just don't know how to tell them the truth. If you take the time to picture your Islands as the circular mixture that we just described, you can also take the time to let your friend in on your secret before you say a word to them, thus cushioning the blow.

Begin this exercise by conjuring a strong image of your Islands and their combination of colors. Close your eyes if you must, and envision your friend physically. Once this picture is clear to you, allow part of the original color you associated with each of your Islands to reach out to your friend. See each of the energies that had once formed your Islands, forming new Islands within your friend. When you are first picturing this, each of your friend's Islands should be one color. Note that the colors may differ from your own once they reach your friend. This is perfectly fine, as you should expect your friends islands to differ from yours somewhat.

When you have created full Islands within the image of your friend, begin to blend them as you did your own until all of the Islands contain all of the original colors. Then, very slowly, pull your friend's energies and your own energies to a point somewhere between the two of you. This does not mean that you have to literally measure out the mid-point between your physical bodies. What you must do is create a central meeting point for your energies as you picture them. If you need to imagine your body standing next to your friend's in order to do this, this is perfectly allowable.

See your energy and your friend's energy meeting with, and then mixing with one another's. Begin by mixing similar colors with one another. Then blend those colors that may be different. Be certain not to allow any color to obliterate another. Blend these colors somewhere between the two of you until each of your Islands and each of your friend's Islands contains all of the colors with which you have been working. When you feel confident that you have blended them as they should be, move all of this energy back toward your self. Picture what it is that you need to tell your friend, and feel happiness blending with your energy as you tell her. Convey your true feelings, and picture your friend understanding why you did what you did, even though she might react with anger or sadness at first. Be sure to picture the end result in a way that creates true happiness for you as well as your friend. You will know that your friend is experiencing true happiness because you are in tune with her energies. And being in tune with these energies ensures that you cannot be entirely selfish and demand happiness for yourself only.

Once you feel that you have envisioned the desired happiness for all involved, and blended this with your own energy, transfer the energy to your friend. Imagine all of the feelings and desires that you created within this energy moving toward the image of your friend. Connect these energies to her Islands and picture the way she reacts to this situation. Make sure it works out happily for both of you in the end.

Although this will not substitute for speaking with your friend physically, it will produce amazing results for you when you do finally speak with her. If this exercise is done correctly, you will have established a connection with your friend that allows her to know the basis of the problem at some level before you even tell her that there is a problem. Being forewarned allows your friend to take the time necessary to develop understanding, and not react in a way that she would inevitably regret later. By forging the connection that you did, you not only managed to cushion the blow, but you told your friend, in a sense, that you were truly desirous of a happy reconciliation for the two of you. When you did finally approach your friend, she already felt this within her.

Exercises such as this one can work wonders in many different areas. To see the results for yourself, all you have to do is try. But connecting your energies with other human beings is not the only way that you can learn from the Island of Nothingness. This next exercise will allow you to reach beyond even this.

Did you ever meet people who seemed to have a gift for communicating with animals? Did they appear to know what a particular dog, cat, or other animal wanted based upon the animal's actions or expression?

Contrary to what many of us learned as we aged, this type of behavior does not occur as the result of the animal being "trained" properly. If an animal is considered "good" or "cute", it is usually because they have demonstrated some form of human-like behavior. Whether this means that they know how to tap you on the arm when they need something, or they simply have expressive eyes, the fact is, they have taken the steps necessary to communicate with you. If you share your life with an animal that you think is not very intelligent, take the time to examine their behavior over the next few days. Notice what they do at certain times of the day. Note the expression on their face, or in their eyes as they perform these actions. Then go through the steps mentioned earlier, and connect to your animal as you would your friend. Begin to sense the way the environment feels from the animal's perspective. If you can, sit near your pet when you form these connections. The benefit of nearness is that you will be able to tell within a short amount of time that this exercise is working. You will not only begin to feel what the animal needs and wants, but you will notice that your pet responds to you in a way that he had not before. Your pet may maintain eye-contact longer, he may become more playful, etc. This is because the animal senses that you are now willing to work with him for better communication. A listless, bored pet is almost always the result of them realizing that your communication connections are shut off. To establish a better relationship with your pet, a friend's pet, or any animal, requires this type of connection. More often than not, those individuals who do not like animals, feel this way because of a lack of connection to them. Those who abuse animals also do not have a connection to them. These individuals do not fully understand the importance of the development of their Islands of Nothingness. They have been taught, or have come to the belief on their own, that human-beings are to be considered separate from animals. Because they are not in touch with their Islands of Nothingness, they do not understand that true happiness occurs when we let go of the belief in separateness, and learn how to connect.

The transference of energies that takes place between all things, can provide us with all that we need to be truly happy. It is false to believe that we each must rely solely on ourselves to provide all that we need. Through the Island of Nothingness, we learn that we get what we truly need and want when we learn to let go of separateness, and exist in a world that we created by connections. The more you practice these exercises, the better you will become at understanding your self and those with whom you have formed connections. And the more you connect with your pet, or any animal, the more intelligent the animal will seem since you now know what it takes to understand her/him. This is all the result of taking the steps necessary to connect with your Island of Nothingness.

Do not think that once you have established connections with other human-beings and animals, that you have fully developed the Island of Nothingness. Look around you at the many different elements that exist in your environment. By using these exercises to connect with plants, you will develop a "green-thumb". If you plan on building a wall of stone, you will be able to tap into the energy associated with particular types of stone, and find the one that is best suited to the environment.

If what we have just described sounds foreign to you, do not despair. We are sure that you are already experiencing these feelings on subtler levels, and a conscious connection to them will only add to your development. Let us give you an example.

Suppose you are buying a multi-vitamin for yourself. (We use this as an example because vitamins and minerals are found in products of the earth.) You go to the store and look at the many different kinds that fill the shelves. You choose a few and look at the labels. Whether someone has recommended a certain brand, or you have already made up your mind that you are going to make your own choice, you quickly become overwhelmed by the vast selection available to you. But as you read the labels on each bottle, you suddenly become aware that certain ingredients sound better to you than others. Although you know little about the vitamins and minerals within each tablet, something inside of you tells you that certain ingredients and percentages would be more beneficial to you than others. If you doubt what you are sensing, and prefer to stay with the brand that another individual recommended to you, you are denying the communication you are receiving from these elements. If, on the other hand, you choose the brand you do based upon knowing that a particular brand *feels* right for you, you have been true to yourself and have recognized your connections.

The previous example explains what happens when you choose to listen to your connections made through the Island of Nothingness, and it also explains what happens when you choose to deny or doubt this Truth. Although we chose to use a vitamin as our example, we are positive that if you think it over, you will remember countless situations in which you have experienced these same feelings. Perhaps you were scheduled to have tests performed by a particular doctor, but changed doctors at the last minute because you kept feeling a sense of dread or discomfort. Suddenly, after you changed doctors, you felt much better. Or perhaps you were told to use a particular pill for a cold. You might have sensed that this was not the right one for you, but chose to rely fully on another's advice without making connections to them to understand why they chose this pill for you. Within a day you discovered that your "instincts" were correct, and this was not the correct pill for you to take. You relied on connections made with others, or the elements that made up a different pill, or even the bacteria which made you sick, and finally made a choice that helped you regain your health. These examples are meant to help you identify the times that connections are made, although you may not be not fully aware. Just imagine how much happiness you could encounter if you made a conscious decision to establish these connections.

We feel it is necessary to add another dimension to your ability to connect with what is around you. Although many of you look to form connections with those items that are contained within the world you created, there are many other "worlds" with which you are capable of connecting. If the author of this book did not choose to use the resources available to her, she would not have been able to connect with us, and therefore would not have been able to share these lessons with you. Whether you choose to believe in gods, or goddesses, or angels, or nothing of this kind, you are as capable as any other individual, of forming connections. The first step is realizing that you are not made of a single Island, but of many Islands, whose sands drift back and forth to each other, and to those with whom you forge your connections. If you choose to pray to something, go back over the exercises discussed throughout this book, and establish a stronger connection to that image. If you would like to establish communication with a loved-one who has left the physical form, you can accomplish this through a review of the exercises as well.[1] You may not receive physical verification for your connections, but as long as you maintain the connections to your Islands, you will understand what Truth outside the physical feels like. Remember, whatever you choose to believe, THAT is your Truth; that which will sustain you and provide you with true happiness.

---

1 Be certain to use the same imagery to allow this entity a pathway back to the realm from which they came. Once your own energy levels have advanced through the practice of the exercises found within this book, you will come to sense and understand this necessity. It will not appeal to your heightened sense of Truth to pressure this entity to remain within this earthly realm when there is the need to accomplish so much in other realms. It is important for their own advancement that they work primarily within their own realm. Your connection to them should offer an invitation for a *temporary* visit only. As you sent energy to others in the exercises provided, (through imagery) send the energy that is your loved-one, back to its proper place.

ABOUT THE AUTHOR

Victoria Tunnermann's experience as a gifted Intuitive spans her lifetime. She incorporates this talent into all aspects of her life including her Past Life Counseling services aimed at assisting others in their quest toward personal truth and happiness.

She currently lives in New Jersey with her husband and daughter.

If you would like to contact the author, or would like more information about her counseling services, you may write to her care of Nevermore Services, P.O. Box 530, Whitehouse Station, NJ 08889. (Please include a self-addressed, stamped envelope for reply.) The author will attempt to answer all correspondence, but cannot guarantee all letters can be answered.

Printed in the United States
36524LVS00004B/464